DUDLEY MOORE
AN INFORMAL BIOGRAPHY

DUDLEY MOORE
AN INFORMAL BIOGRAPHY
by Jeff Lenburg

A DELILAH BOOK
Distributed by The Putnam Publishing Group
NEW YORK

A DELILAH BOOK
Delilah Communications Ltd.
118 E. 25 Street
New York, New York 10010

ISBN: 0-933328-56-7
Library of Congress Catalog Card Number: 82-74037

Manufactured in the U.S.A.
First printing 1983

Front Cover Photograph:
Ruan O'Lochlainn/Globe Photos

Front Cover Color Tint:
Marilyn Ward

Back Cover Photo:
R. Dominguez/Globe Photos

Back Cover Design:
Virgina Rubel

Cover and Book Design:
Ed Caraeff

Dedication:

TO MY LOVING GRANDMOTHER, MARY GALICH

Acknowledgments:

Recognition is due the following companies, people and libraries that contributed information, background material, and interview substance for this book: Orion Pictures; Paramount Pictures; 20th Century Fox; *THE TIMES* of London; *THE HOLLYWOOD REPORTER;* and *DAILY VARIETY.*

Then, to the following people who helped above and beyond the call of duty: Mike Lefebvre; Dennis McLellan of the *LOS ANGELES TIMES;* Gwyniver Jones of BBC Written Archives; Bridget Carter of the British Broadcasting Corporation (BBC); Lou Pitt of ICM; Roger Bloch and his staff; Randy Skretvedt (notably for contributing the record soundtracks of *BEYOND THE FRINGE* and *GOOD EVENING);* and Greg Lenburg (thankfully for his proofreading of the final manuscript).

Lastly my tip of the hat to the libraries and staffs of The Academy of Arts and Sciences (Margaret Herrick Library) *THEATRE WORLD; PEOPLE* magazine; and the American Film Institute.

Special thanks to Jeannie Sakol, Richard Amdur, Melissa Smith, Richard Schatzberg, Virginia Rubel, Kathryn Greene, and Vikki DiDonato.

And, of course, my special thanks to Dudley Moore for compelling me to take his music and comedy to heart, as this biography bears out.

CHAPTER 1

"Growing Up"

Generally, the life stories of Hollywood's greatest comedians take on a tragic, Charles Dickens-like rags-to-riches theme when chronicled for posterity. The saga of Dudley Moore is no exception. Following an unhappy childhood, years of struggle through two disastrous marriages and near-obscurity, he has rebounded, and, like a proud lion, burst onto the entertainment scene to feast on the fruits of success.

Moore's early triumphs were the kind audiences quickly forgot, even if reasonably successful, since many of them originated in England and were only later given some play in America. He recorded several million-seller record albums in England with British comedian Peter Cook. He headlined (also with Cook) in the 1960s and 1970s in two smash London and Broadway stage revues, *BEYOND THE FRINGE* and *GOOD EVENING*. Moore appeared in nearly half-a-dozen British comedy films and wrote jingles for television. Despite this impressive array of credits, Dudley fell into oblivion until his performances in such box-office gems as *10* (with Bo Derek) and *ARTHUR* caught the fancy of millions of filmgoers the world over, finally putting him in the limelight to stay.

Dudley is that rarity in the show business world: the multi-talented man who can act, play the piano, violin, and organ, write music, and perform physical comedy. Oh, yes, women also figure among his leading triumphs, as his current liaison with actress/model Susan Anton attests. Most of all, though, it is Dudley's comedy that has meant his worldwide success—he is a slapstick master in the tradition of Laurel and Hardy, Charlie Chaplin, Buster Keaton, Peter Sellers and Jerry Lewis, a comic wordsmith in the typically British way, and a fresh presence with a style all his own.

What is most surprising about Dudley is that he never intended to become a comedian! Music was always his true love, and at first he pursued a full-time professional musical career, leaving any ambitions to become an actor and comedian last on his list of priorities.

To understand what makes Dudley so likeable and popular today, one needs to comprehend the tremendous amount of personal adversity he overcame to reach his place atop the heap of film comedians. Moore was born with a club foot to Ada Francis (a secretary) and John Moore (a railroad electrician) at the local hospital in Dagenham, Essex, on April 19, 1935. Dudley's parents were both from devoutly religious stocks: Ada was the daughter of a faith healer who wrote books on Christian Science, and John was an Anglo-Catholic. Religion, however, did not play a major role in Dudley's life. Rather, the most important influence seems to have been his diminutive height. At 5 feet, 2 inches, Moore was the shortest member of the family. Growing up, by his own recollection, meant "undergoing a series of operations on my foot and wondering whether I would ever grow taller."

While the other children in Dudley's small working-class community were going to school and learning to play soccer, almost every English lad's favorite sport, Dudley spent most of his time visiting hospitals to be treated for his damaged leg. At times, he remembered, he was the "only boy in a ward full of screaming soldiers." Moore has also vividly recalled that his sixth Christmas was spent in a local convalescent home recuperating from his sixth operation. "A nurse, Pat her name was, came to tuck me in bed. I was terribly frightened and alone and she said, 'Do you want me to kiss you goodnight?' I said, 'No.' Then, she said, 'Okay,' and walked away until I shouted after her, 'Yes,' and she came back and kissed me. I will never forget her. She was a woman who was really an example of free love," Moore said.

Although the operations were relatively successful, Dudley never grew another inch. He frequently asked his mother if his height would ever change but, as he remembers, "My mother always said, 'Don't worry, dear, you'll be as big as Uncle Bernard.' That didn't help because Uncle Bernard was only 5 feet 8. My parents were about the same size as I am, and my sister, Barbara, was the one who grew to 5 feet 8. We made very funny family photographs together." Predictably, schoolmates saw the dwarfish Dudley as an easy target and rarely stopped teasing and bullying him. Dudley grew tired of this abuse and, preferring not to wage a probably-losing battle against his taller adversaries, developed a sharp and wonderful wit with which to stifle the merciless attacks. As Dudley says today, "Being short certainly interfered with my life. It would have been difficult to beat up on someone who was taller than me. So I developed my humor. I became sadistic with my humor, and, with that tool, I knew I could cut others down to size." Dudley's talent for jesting put a quick stop to the taunts of his foes.

Ironically, Dudley's intelligence and his capacity to think quickly caused new problems: "If you show yourself to be good at something in school, you risk being unpopular with kids who don't find that attractive. That's what kept me from pushing ahead. There were other kids like that in the classroom, but I don't even remember them. I only remember the kids who used to beat me up during lunch hour," says Moore.

Those pestering schoolkids who did so much for Dudley's sense of humor also inspired him, at age six, to vent his aggressions in another way: through music. Although Dudley credits his mother for influencing him to try music (hers was a musical family as well), he once remarked that his small size aided the development of his multiple talents. "I had a real hang up about being short, and was very shy and lacking in confidence. When I was at school, I couldn't impress people by playing rugby, so I tried to entertain and make them laugh."

Emboldened by a powerful wit and harboring an increasing interest in music, Dudley's confidence grew. He began to spend much time after school practicing the piano with his favorite book of music, which, resplendent in a purple binding, contained such Victorian melodies as "March Militaire" and "Robin's Return." Soon he began entertaining family and friends with occasional at-home concerts, and by the time he was eight years old had turned to jazz as his favorite kind of music. Dudley was also a member of the church choir, playing the organ and singing with the ensemble, until his interest in these activities began to fade, along with his religious beliefs.

By age 11, his dreams had undergone another metamorphosis. Now desiring to become a concert violinist, Dudley was awarded a scholarship to the Guildhall School of Music, where he widened his repertoire by learning to play the violin, organ, and harpsichord, as well as mastering his studies of musical theory and composition. His parents, though poor, scraped up enough money to buy Dudley his first violin. In remembering the acquisition of the instrument, Moore once said, "I was so desperate to play the violin, to do it well, that I wasn't any good at it. It took quite a while before I realized this and went back to working on the piano." Two years later, he began to play the piano at weddings for a five-guinea fee (about $15), which, for a teen-ager in 1948, was a small fortune. Moore remembers his constant trips to the music store that served as an added inspiration towards becoming a jazz pianist: "There was one music shop near me in Ilford, and I would pick up whatever I could there—song sheets of the odd George Shearing, a bit of Fats Waller. But Errol Garner became a great influence on me."

Occasionally, Dudley dabbled in the theatre, acting as an angel in a Christmas pageant, and in languages by studying French and Italian. But he always returned to music. And although classical music was of great interest to him, Dudley found that jazz, with its heavy rhythms, could maintain his passion for music forever. Moore has admitted to having another strong motivation for choosing to become a musician; he reasoned that many musicians find their jazz playing accompanied by women. So, with an admiration for music and women already well developed, Dudley, by age 17, was devoting most of his time to playing the organ.

His musical precocity soon won him a scholarship to study the organ at Magdalen College, an affiliate of Oxford University, where Dudley received his B.A. degree in music in 1957, followed by an additional degree in composition in 1958. His classmates again posed problems—they resented the fact that Moore, a member of the working-class, had been admitted into the college. Traditionally, students attending Oxford were sons of nobility or captains of industry, and did not come from such "ordinary" backgrounds as Moore's.

Because Dudley had become accustomed to being teased, he paid little attention to his classmates' insensitivity, and later remarked, "They thought I talked funny— funny, strange, not funny—and I regarded them the same way. There was one fellow in my class who was so refined that his lips never moved when he spoke." To keep working in the face of all this animosity, Moore kept one vision in mind as his incentive. "I was fascinated by the image of some luscious creature leaning across the piano while I played, whispering requests, and overtures," Dudley confessed. Unfortunately, no such woman ever materialized. Unbowed, Dudley continued to strive ahead by playing in local cabarets and writing music for plays in which he occasionally acted.

During his tenure at Oxford, Moore also became notorious in a relatively short span of time as the university's Clown Prince, famous for his musical parodies and his guile as a performer. In a humorous school production of *THE BIRDS*, Dudley treated the audience to one of his western send-ups, singing in an unnerving falsetto. In another brief appearance in an open-air theatre production, *BARTHOLOMEW FAIR*, Moore strolled across the stage crying, "Apples, apples, who'll buy my lovely apples?" Taking a small bite out of the fruit, he suddenly appeared confused over its identity, and began his sing-song again, but with a minor correction: "Pears, pears, who'll buy my lovely pears." Even at this early stage of his career, Dudley displayed a deft sense of humor.

Though Moore suffered from the same insecurities at Oxford as he had experienced as a child in grammar school, Dudley found that acting gave him the necessary confidence to prevail. He proved himself in several dramatic productions, performing characters such as Enobarbus, Autolycus, Offenbach's Orpheus, and as a deaf mute in *THE CHANGELING*. His masterful performances won the plaudits of his drama professors as well as the respect of his classroom allies.

After his graduation from Oxford in 1958, Dudley was faced with the imposing task of finding some kind of regular work. Dudley's first jobs consisted of composing music for ballets and television commercials, and while this was not really what he wanted to be doing, he hoped that these tireless efforts would eventually lead him to something more permanent. Like many university graduates, Moore was unsure of what his future held in store. He could only keep his chin up high and hope for the best.

Dudley Moore, Cleo Laine and her husband John Dankworth, 1959.

CHAPTER 2

"The Outer 'Fringes' of Moore"

Dudley plugged diligently away at anchoring his roots as a professional jazz musician, since music meant everything to him—status, women, money, and more women. Dudley's first break came when he signed on with the Vic Lewis Orchestra, which was en route to America to play at various armed forces camps. Remembering his first exposure to the life of a musician, Dudley quipped, "I finally hit the big time. They put me up at the YMCA." Actually, Moore considers his first major musical concert tour an ecstatic time of unforgettable pleasure, not nearly as disastrous as he likes to claim. GI's rollicked to the brassy sounds of the Vic Lewis Orchestra, and swung to a melange of their jazz melodies. Amid the clusters of saxophones and trombones, Dudley could be seen pounding almost effortlessly on the ivory keys of his piano in the bravura style of his childhood idol, Errol Garner, the famous English musician. This series of concert engagements provided a unique opportunity for Dudley to play professionally and test his polished jazz skills in public.

Dudley credits two musical contemporaries, John Dankworth and Cleo Laine, for helping him to land the job with the Lewis band. "I was playing at a May ball in 1958 when they (John and Cleo) came to hear me. John recommended me for a job with the Vic Lewis Orchestra. In fact, it was with Vic that I *first* came to America, " Moore recounted. Young Dudley clearly enjoyed his first magical musical tour and never wanted it to end. The constant roar of army G.I.'s caught up in jazz fever was enough to send Moore into a transcendental state of happiness, and made him hope that he could savor the cheers with the Vic Lewis band a little longer. But after the band's final army base appearance in New York, Lewis decided to take the band back to England.

Lewis, however, was unable to convince one hold-out to return with him: Dudley Moore, who felt his musical mission in America was not quite complete. Although Moore initially found himself strapped for employment (New York City was inundated at the time by hordes of aspiring jazz musicians who saw the city as a kind of mecca), it was not long before he teamed up with a trio of musicians and managed to finagle a booking at the Village Vanguard, a swank Manhattan nightclub. The Moore jazz combo played nightly for a short time and showcased Dudley's keyboard abilities to audiences who had never seen or heard of him before. These exhilarating performances by Dudley soon became the highlight of the band's performance, and remained as such for the duration of its engagement. A member of the enthusiastic audience one evening, Ahmet Ertegun of Atlantic Records, was acting as a scout to find new recording talent. As Moore and his band's time at the Vanguard grew short, Ertegun paid the comedian-musician a surprise visit backstage after the final performance. Ertegun was quite impressed with the comedian's musical dexterity and wanted to sign Dudley to a recording contract. But Moore, feeling homesick and probably a little fearful, declined and took the first plane back to England.

It was apparent that Dudley lacked the necessary confidence in himself to succeed on his own; and while he didn't mind performing as an integral part of a musical group, Dudley was still a meek, shy nervous soul not mentally ready for the life of a soloist. He estimated that his outlook would change once he was back in the familiar environs of Dagenham with old friends like musician John Dankworth. Dudley contacted Dankworth, who had since formed his own jazz band, and the popular jazz conductor/composer, remembering the formidable talent of his shy friend, didn't hestitate to add Dudley to the ensemble.

A grateful Moore never passed up an opportunity to show Dankworth that he hadn't made a mistake. For nine solid months, Moore earned his keep playing gig after gig with the John Dankworth Band. But Dudley had one apparent phobia: "I was a bit nervous about playing behind the soloists, because at the time I was on a terrific Errol Garner kick. I played in his style even when the other musicians were trying to make a chorus, and they felt it was impossible to solo against me." Moore perceived the other musicians' reluctance to compete with his virtuoso performances as personal accolades, thereby boosting his shaky self-confidence.

In a matter of time, Dudley had gained so much self-esteem that he decided to leave the Dankworth jazz band and try working up a comic-musicians' act of his own at local nightclubs and cabarets. And though the nightspots themselves may have been familiar to Dudley—his early dates were at clubs on the outskirts of his hometown, Dagenham—learning the ropes of a comedian was untested, foreign territory that presented its share of obstacles.

Luckily, the irrepressible crackling wit that served Moore so well as a child proved to be a welcome addition to his act. Moore held his own on stage, with a pleasant combination of one-liners, stories, and piano-playing, but found that doing comedy required the kind of discipline and training he had never enjoyed. He has often admitted since then that he wasn't fond of preparations and rehearsals, preferring instead to work with the strengths of his instincts and improvisational skills.

Moore's act was reminiscent of another great and widely acclaimed piano satirist, Victor Borge. But as Moore eventually found out, life as a nightclub singer not only turned into a humbling experience, it became the lowest ebb of his career. One night, while playing at a Manchester club, Dudley found himself pitted on the same bill against a team of wrestlers and striptease artists. Since the gritty performances of the wrestlers boosted pub sales, while the seductive strippers pleased the sexual tastes of the male crowd, these were exceedingly difficult acts for Dudley to follow. His appearance as a sophisticated comic-musician was simply no match for the more visceral pleasures inspired and desired by the low-brow assembly, and so, his act fizzled as fast as the suds on patrons' beers. As Dudley recalls, "No one warned me what a dive it was. So after the strippers went off, I came out and did a brilliant satire on Schubert's lieder songs and some of the more obscure operas of Benjamin Britten." The wit of Moore's material went completely unnoticed and he bombed miserably.

Despite this debacle, Dudley continued, using the same material in subsequent cabaret performances. Following a change of venue, audiences became more receptive to his performances, and it appeared the chance would finally begin to pay off. Just around the corner was the major breakthrough that Dudley had been waiting for.

A youthful Dudley at the piano, 1960.

PLAYBILL
the magazine for theatregoers

BEYOND THE FRINGE

In 1960, at the behest of Scotland's famed Edinburgh Festival, Dudley joined with Peter Cook, Jonathan Miller, and Alan Bennett in creating a satirical stage revue, *BEYOND THE FRINGE*. Besides Moore, Cook was the only other comedian out of the four. Bennett and Miller were both college graduates and non-professional actors. The result: an outrageously funny show that rapidly moved to London as a powerful, revolutionary comedy revue, opening at the Fortune Theatre on May 10, 1961. The show drew thousands of theatregoers and tremendous critical acclaim during its two year knockout engagement in London, whereupon the show moved to Broadway and equaled its own success.

Peter Cook remembers that one of the festival's producers, John Bassett, was responsible for seeking out the services of this British foursome. As Cook tells it: "He was looking for a late night revue. They'd had Flanders and Swann the year before. And he knew Dudley personally, he knew Jonathan, and he'd heard of me. In fact, he asked Jonathan and Dudley to suggest two other people—one from Oxford and another from Cambridge. Jonathan suggested me."

Prior to the show's London premiere, Dudley, Bennett, and Miller signed contracts for the show, each receiving one hundred pounds a piece ($170 by today's exchange rate). Only Peter Cook held out. "I was the only one with an agent," Cook says. "He advised me against doing the show. He said it would be an amateur revue and that I'd spoil my status as a professional. I finally decided to do it anyway. The others were to get 100 pounds to do it, but my agent insisted that I get more. So I got 110 pounds. Of course, my agent took ten percent, leaving me with only 99 pounds."

BEYOND THE FRINGE swiftly rose above its amateur status to become the craziest stage revue since two American comedians, Olsen and Johnson, invaded Broadway with their long-running show, *SONS O' FUN*, in the 1940s. Like the Olsen and Johnson hit, *BEYOND THE FRINGE* was comprised of a series of comedy sketches, each one an integral part of an overall theme which good-naturedly lampooned British protocol. The show broke all London house records and quickly made Dudley Moore a familiar character to many theatregoers. Then, riding the crest of its success, *BEYOND THE FRINGE* moved to America.

Retaining its original cast, the show arrived in September 1962 for brief engagements in Washington, D.C., Boston, and Toronto, Canada, prior to its Broadway premiere at New York City's John Golden Theatre on October 27. The show was comprised of twenty-two sketches and was directed by English stage veteran Eleanor

Jonathan Miller, Peter Cook, Alan Bennett and a mournful Dudley Moore in "Beyond the Fringe," 1961.

Fazan, with the troupe's off-beat humor and outrageous word play reminding theatregoers of the Marx Brothers, England's Goons, and Abbott and Costello (especially their famous "Who's On First?" routine), all rolled up into one human laugh-making machine.

In *BEYOND THE FRINGE*, Dudley's comic prowess was never more certain. Audiences shook the theatre's rafters with laughter and delight over his comic antics, reveled in his playful musical parodies, and helped propel his career to new heights. Of Dudley's performance in particular, a critic for *THE TIMES* of London wrote: "Mr. Dudley Moore is something of a virtuoso on the piano and is well able to hold the audience with a piece of playing that rises swiftly to a thundering climax and then finds no way of coming to a stop. Mr. Moore is extremely droll as he struggles desperately with power-

ful music which has taken the bit between its teeth."

Moore's involvement with the production, however, was actually rather limited, as he once explained: "It was the easiest physical job I have ever done—wandering on and off stage—just terrific to do." What Dudley meant was he never stayed on stage for more than two segments at a time, so the audience never had time to tire of his, or his contemporaries', antics. These madcap stage routines saw Moore truly in command for the first time in his life, not only with his career but with his personal vision of where he was heading. Gone were the frustration and daily anxiety that seemed to plague his climb up the ladder of success. Gone were the sleepless nights, and the unceasing speculation as to what the future would hold. Dudley, at least temporarily, had broken out of his shell and walked the stage with vigor and confidence.

Alan Bennett (with glasses), always a professorial-looking chap, was studying Russian history at Oxford University when the surprise offer came to join the three other college cut-ups for the Beyond the Fringe *revue. He quickly established a reputation among the four for being the most erudite and astute observer of the English scene, and never failed to impress his cohorts with a talent for expounding on any given topic. He so nurtured these skills of observation and deftness with language over the years that he is now widely acknowledged as one of the most important playwrights in England (a distinction that has earned him numerous awards). Bennett's significant works of drama and satire include* The Old Country *(which starred Alec Guinness),* Habeas Corpus, *and* Forty Years On, *all proving that his calling in life was not as a Kremlinologist but to pen his special brand of social commentary.*

While Peter Cook (second from left) has not achieved the American-style super-stardom won by his chum, Dudley Moore, in England he is every bit the star that Moore is. His Cambridge University career as King of the undergraduate comedy revue scene led to his hijinks in Beyond the Fringe. *A decade long partnership with "Dud" followed, an association that etched a permanent niche in the world of humor on two continents. Cook is a perennially popular sight on both BBC television and in England's gossip columns. As Dudley once wrote about him: "I cannot conceive of working with someone with a more royally precise sense of timing and character."*

The urbane and dynamic Jonathan Miller (third from left) is a breathtaking mix of artist, satirist, scientist and wit, an all around original thinker. His foray into farce with Beyond the Fringe *steered him away form his Cambridge University studies of neuropathology; though he did earn the title of Dr. Miller, he followed a more theatrical path instead. Miller has directed many controversial renditions of the plays of William Shakespeare for the BBC, written and hosted a highly-acclaimed BBC science special called* THE BODY IN QUESTION, *and lectured at major English universities. The myriad talents displayed by this contemporary virtuoso have truly earned Jonathan Miller the epithet "modern day Renaissance man."*

In New York, *BEYOND THE FRINGE* continued playing to sellout crowd after sellout crowd, with tickets almost as difficult to find as they would be for a New York Yankees' World Series game. In celebration of the show's prolonged success, producer-director Alexander H. Cohen decided to update the show before its opening for a fifth consecutive year. His changes secured, *BEYOND THE FRINGE '64* made its debut on January 8, 1964 at the John Golden Theatre, featuring a new format of comedy material (written by Dudley Moore, Alan Bennett, Peter Cook, and Jonathan Miller) and the same cast of comic regulars (Paxton Whitehead occasionally spelled Jonathan Miller). Moreover, the second edition of this British comedy revue was wilder, funnier, more exaggerated, and madder than its popular predecessor.

Unlike the first edition of this English stage revue, *BEYOND THE FRINGE '64* concentrated on American issues rather than British and was more timely than the original. Americans were still mourning the tragic assassination of President John F. Kennedy and, perhaps, needed to laugh more than ever before. *BEYOND THE FRINGE '64* was welcome comic relief indeed, not only for Broadway theatregoers, but for comedy lovers in general.

As *BEYOND THE FRINGE '64* opens, Dudley is playing the piano to the tune of America's national anthem, "The Star Spangled Banner," with Cook, Bennett, and Miller comically humming along. At the conclusion of Moore's piano harmony the British comedians begin poking fun at America and its traditions in their sketch, "Home Thoughts Abroad." Of the surging problem of black Americans, Dudley says, "I gather the colored people are *sweeping* the country." John, eyes bulging, wisely quips, "They are. It's one of the few jobs they can get!" Comic confusion continues to surface on other black American issues when Dudley queries, "What's all this black muslin I hear they're wearing?" Peter, never one to miss a comic cue, remarks, "They're not wearing it, they're *joining* it. It's a movement—not a cloth." Poverty in America is also scrutinized when Cook flatly states, "It's [the poverty] all been concentrated in the slum areas. It's beautifully done. You would scarcely notice it." Changing the subject, Miller makes an astute observation concerning America's sexual naivete, particularly the way many men would be happier if all women possessed the same physical attributes, mainly blonde hair and huge breasts. Bennett casually interjects that English males don't think of sex in the same manner, not as *pathetically* as Americans seem to do. Cook, wanting to discern how his esteemed compatriots view the opposite gender, asks how they picture sexy women. Dudley replies, "I try not to—otherwise I start thinking of beautiful women with huge breasts and pink skins . . ." They all four chime in, "Pink skins, yes . . . yes . . . pathetic . . . absolutely pathetic."

In "The English Way of Death," Alan Bennett portrays a frail, senile old woman explaining that cremation seems to her the most proper mode of burial, even though one can never be certain that the immediate family will get the ashes of the right person. ("For all you know, it might be a couple of copies of t'*Yorkshire Evening Post* they burnt up.") As he wryly adds later, . . . "It's more hygienic. And I think there's a lot less palaver about t'service up at t'crematorium. It only takes ten minutes. I mean you go in there like and you hear abait of music—Handel's Largo or summat like that, then t'parson says a few words like and then t'coffin goes through and you come out. And do you know, there's folks waitin' to get in, they're that busy."

As a change of pace from the comic morbidity of this sketch, Dudley offered his musical parody, "The Ballad of Gangster Joe," a nonsensical ditty sung in a thick German accent, while mugging at the audience for laughs. Later in the show, in a hilarious sketch called "The Royal Box," Dudley portrays a drama enthusiast bent on meeting the Royal Family at a London theatre in their royal box seats (he's seen the same production almost *500* times in anticipation of their appearance!) And in "One Leg Too Few" Dudley plays Mr. Spiggot, a one-legged actor trying out for the role of Tarzan. Cook, cast in the role of straight man and movie producer, tactlessly explains to Spiggot that he hasn't got a chance to win the part of the vine-swinging hero unless he sprouts another leg (or, as he put it more thoughtfully later, "You are deficient in the leg division to the tune of one"). Spiggot's only chance to land the movie role, Cook says, would be if no *two*-legged individuals applied. Since there seems a slim chance of that happening, Spiggot thanks Cook, and hops offstage with his one-legged gait.

Dudley revealed in an interview that the sketch was his idea and that it was also used in another London stage production entitled, *PIECES OF EIGHT*. Moore was surprised that Cook and he were able to perform the risqué skit at all.

Dudley also appeared in the show as an English Lord in "Lord Cobbold, The Duke," wherein he is teamed once more with Peter Cook. This time, the subject is theatrical censorship, with Cook acting as interviewer to Moore's "man on the street" character. Dudley maintains that there is too much sex and violence in these productions already and that "I don't want to see lust, rape, incest and sodomy. I can get all that at home."

Other highlights of the show include "A Piece of My Mind," featuring Jonathan Miller commenting on the insoluble problem of trouser-stealing criminals, and "The Great Train Robbery," in which a bemused Alan Bennett conducts a televison interview with Peter Cook as a Scotland Yard police chief. One of the verbal gems that Cook proffers during this skit: "When you speak of a train robbery, this involved *no* loss of train...we haven't lost a train since 1946, I believe it was—the year of the great snows when we mislaid a small one."

BEYOND THE FRINGE '64 ranked among critics' favorite Broadway shows for the years 1964 and 1965, for many more good reasons than could be listed here. The British foursome brought to Broadway, for 669 performances, the kind of high-level lunacy and dark comedy farce that had been clearly missing from the stage for quite some time. Because of the show's astronomical success, Moore, Cook, Bennett, and Miller were no longer just a bunch of unknown amateurs. They had risen to the plateau of comedians supreme, able to pursue even greater challenges. Yet, such was not to be the calling for all involved.

As New York started preparing for a new Broadway season, Cook, Moore, Bennett, and Miller went their separate ways. Only Cook and Moore were determined to make a career out of show business. Jonathan Miller was already practicing medicine as a doctor on the side and intended to return to pathology. Alan Bennett, meanwhile, decided to take up his former work as a lecturer, student of, and writer about medieval history. Since Peter Cook had no desire to remain in New York either, he returned to England and planned to remain idle for at least six months. And Dudley? He stayed in the United States for a time to work at nightclubs and with the Boston Arts Festival production of *EMPEROR JONES,* assisting with music and choreography. (Earlier, in 1963, Moore also broke from production of *BEYOND THE FRINGE* to work out the musical arrangements for dancer/choreographer Gillian Lynne's London stage version of *THE OWL AND THE PUSSYCAT.*)

Dudley was, apparently, content with the idea of pursuing his professional music career, mixing comedy with jazz piano as part of his single's act. To Moore, working on stage in local cabarets was the kind of work he enjoyed most, since each performance was like fulfilling a lifelong dream. "I try creating a good feeling whether I'm performing on stage or on the piano," Moore stated at the time. "To me, it's the most ecstatic feeling."

Shortly after the *BEYOND THE FRINGE* quartet broke-up, Dudley was given the next great offer of his young career: his own fortnightly BBC televison show, *NOT ONLY...BUT ALSO,* teaming him with none other than Peter Cook. Since America had little to offer him at the moment, Moore was pleased that an English television producer thought him worthy of his own series. Dudley wasted no time in moving back to London to start rehearsals for the show, which made its BBC debut on January 9, 1965. Besides marking the official start of the Cook and Moore partnership, *NOT ONLY...BUT ALSO* represents the origin of the comedians' most popular characters, Pete and Dud, two brainless, self-indulgent

Moore and Cook from the "One Leg Too Few" sketch in "Beyond the Fringe '64."

gentlemen who enjoy reveling in the world of their own fantasies. Their musings centered around, among other things, women, sex, women, subjects of news-making interest, and women.

Pete and Dud were unquestionably the show's biggest hits. In one typical episode, Pete and Dud are riding together on a bus, exchanging reminiscences in Walter Mitty fashion about women in their lives. They try convincing each other through their lurid recollections just how many tender, loving moments they've had with women, when actually their sex lives have been grossly disappointing.

Basically, the duo's sketches combined slapstick with topical social commentary, exemplified in a skit wherein Cook and Moore poke fun at the absurdities of the business world. A personnel officer (Peter Cook) takes a candidate (Dudley Moore) out to lunch in order to assess his qualities and capacities. The conversation gradually becomes an exercise in dementia, with Cook emptying a soup plate over his companion. The ensuing romp was as chaotic as the early Mack Sennett comedies, and though the message may have been hard to find under the layers of soup and slapstick, Cook and Moore were trying to make one point clear; never mix business with pleasure! Or soup with nuts!

Along with the wild, perplexing antics of Pete and Dud, Dudley was also featured weekly on the show doing a character of his own creation: Mr. Wistey, a brittle old man garbed in a drab mackintosh and battered hat. Usually, Moore would perform this bizarre character sitting on a park bench, droning deadpan monologues on a variety of outlandish themes. This character rivaled Dud as a cult idol to millions of British viewers, who saw some small kernel of their own idiosyncrasies in this pathetic, little

caricature. Finally, Dudley's renditions of popular jazz melodies on the piano were invaluable to the success of every segment of the show.

A critic for THE TIMES of London newspaper described the series in his review as "immensely funny and clean as a whistle. It is mostly composed and performed by two young men, Mr. Peter Cook and Mr. Dudley Moore, graduates from BEYOND THE FRINGE, who are endowed with a rare talent for devising original comic situations." Gabriela Marik, a critic for Edinburgh's The Scotsman newspaper, touted the show for its "cerebral fun within a framework pitched at a wide and possibly low-brow audience."

Marik couldn't have come closer to the truth when she remarked that NOT ONLY . . . BUT ALSO was targeted for "a low-brow audience"—because it was. Originally, the series was intended to reach out to a smaller audience, and was telecast over the BBC 2 channel, a secondary programming station. But overwhelming audience approval and unanticipated high ratings quickly changed all of that. It was not long before the BBC's main channel picked up the series, which secured NOT ONLY. . . BUT ALSO's domination of BBC telewaves. Then came the immediate order from the station's hierarchy to produce a second season of shows, which began on January 15, 1966. Dudley was now considered one of the hottest show business properties in the United Kingdom.

So naturally, when the second season of NOT ONLY. . . BUT ALSO premiered, Cook and Moore fans were anticipating new sketches featuring their heroes, Pete and Dud. They were not disappointed, although Dudley remarked that he and Cook tried spacing out Pete and Dud skits since they were often very tiring to do. 'I found that I got exhausted whenever I did that sketch," Moore related. "It didn't matter who we were

Moore and Cook as "Pete" and "Dud" from "Not Only . . . But Also."

—Laurel or Hardy or whoever—you had to work at keeping the pace and keeping the energy up." Cook and Moore supplemented the Pete and Dud appearances with a variety of other sketches, one of Dudley's favorites being a spoof of Welsh singer Tom Jones. "Once on television we did a skit with Ludwig Beethoven as Tom Jones," said Dudley, who portrayed Jones singing his hit, "It's Not Unusual," with a Beethoven-German accent. Cook added to the insanity of the sketch with his zany imitation of Francisco Jose de Goya, the celebrated Spanish artist. Together they became a most unusual pair!

The new season of NOT ONLY... BUT ALSO continued to score consistently high ratings on the BBC network and drew both British and Australian television viewers (the latter country was also broadcasting the series). The series, however, met an abrupt and merciless end on February 15, 1966 when the BBC yanked the show off the air. Apparently, Cook and Moore aired one sketch that contained some "objectionable language"—language of the sort that was not permitted on television, but it is still not known exactly what the offending language consisted of.

Dudley was devastated when he received word of the show's cancellation. The series had given his career a gigantic boost and the loss of the weekly national forum came as a blow. Taking the sudden demise of his series in stride, however, Moore fearlessly went on to try another British television venue, the talk show. He enjoys recalling the audience reaction to his first (and perhaps prophetic) appearance in 1965. "I have to confess, with some embarrassment, I became sort of a sex symbol. I was talking about my old girlfriends in school, how obsessed I was with them, and from that moment I was called, 'Cuddly Dudley.'"

Clearly, his sex appeal was potent enough to win over Suzy Kendall, an English actress and former model who became his newest steady companion. In 1965, the same year BEYOND THE FRINGE closed up shop, Dudley began dating Suzy and over a period of several months fell deeply in love with her. Eventually, their relationship became serious and very intimate, so they moved in together. A sultry blonde, 5 feet 4 inches tall, Kendall was no stranger to American and United Kingdom filmgoers. She was especially known for her roles as the school teacher with a crush on Sidney Poitier in To Sir, With Love, the rape victim in The Penthouse, and the poor little rich girl in Up the Junction.

With Dudley now a star, it became increasingly difficult to maintain the privacy of the relationship and keep it from the public, not to mention the British press corps. Moore, fiercely protective of his privacy, became a primary target for scoop-seeking gossip reporters. Happily, the relationship between Dudley and Suzy did not include the headline-making, stormy feuds and petty jealousies that seemed to destroy other celebrity romances, so the occasional item in the columns was never problematic. The couple enjoyed each other's company and seemed never able to spend enough time together, prompting their purchase of a 230-year-old brick house in Hampstead, in northern London. The mansion and its grounds contained all the grace and charm of a small castle, featuring seven rooms and with part of the foundation built around a tree trunk. Even the basement had a special, unusual accessory: an underground running spring.

In an interview, Kendall once recalled what happened in her early days with Dudley. "Dudley moved in with me about four months after we met. I had been living with a girl friend and we lived in that apart-

Suzy Kendall and Dudley Moore, 1969.

ment for a year and a half after she moved out, before we bought the house," Kendall said. Dudley was not Suzy's only constant companion at the Hampstead spread: five Persian cats, Charlie, Sadie (named after the legendary Sadie Thompson), Ada (sporting the moniker of Dudley's mother), and two without any name at all filled out the Moore household. Suzy admits that she couldn't stand being separated from Dudley for more than a week at a time, and stayed home with him when she could, playing Ping-Pong, sleeping, or just relaxing in general. Oc-

casionally, Dudley would take Suzy for a spin in his black Maserati, or in Kendall's own yellow Jaguar-E, to spice up their indoor routine.

Dudley and Suzy had no immediate marriage plans, even in the event of the birth of a child. When asked what his reaction to children would be, Dudley responded in a timely interview, "If they arrive, jolly good. But so far they haven't and I'm beginning to wonder if perhaps I have a chemical deficiency in me—like too much ginger beer!" Dudley, in keeping with his opportunistic

Moore and Cook in "Not Only . . . But Also," 1970.

sense of comedic timing, was unable to resist turning a serious moment into a whimsical one. Kendall, however, later expanded upon Moore's sentiments to add that they were very happy without being married and that their parents approved of their live-in relationship. Suzy's first marriage to a jazz musician had ended in divorce, and she felt no urge to hurry her relationship with Dudley to the altar.

Likewise, Dudley was unready to exchange marriage vows so quickly and instead encouraged Suzy to pursue her own career ambitions as an actress, while he contemplated his next career move.

Moore had already conquered the realm of the theatre with *BEYOND THE FRINGE* and the medium of television with his own weekly series. He wanted to maintain his partnership with Peter Cook as a quasi-comedy team. But Moore's truly burning desire was to challenge another alien territory: motion pictures, wherein he would hopefully be able to fully utilize every aspect of his diverse talent. The only problem, as he saw it, was waiting for the right offer to materialize.

CHAPTER 3

"The Comedy Team, Cook and Moore"

Since it was Dudley's wish to become recognized as a full-fledged comedian, in 1965 he focused his attention on career inroads other than musical playdates and television guest appearances. Moore's long and successful tour with the BEYOND THE FRINGE comedy troupe provided him with the realization that he possessed that rare gift: the art of making people laugh. So Dudley and Peter Cook formed a team with the hopes of one day breaking into the cinematic scene together, to follow the footsteps of many great comedy teams before them.

Their partnership soon caught fire and they were compared to those Hollywood immortals, Abbott and Costello. When they weren't recreating their infamous television personae Pete and Dud, Cook's role was as Moore's mentor whose job it was, as the straight man, to steer Dudley's lunatic performances back on the right track. But Peter's subtle devices were different from the domineering, grossly overbearing straight man/boss character that had become common in many American comedy teams. Instead, Cook relied on his dry wit, comic

finesse, and a genteel, dignified approach to redefine Moore's boundaries and keep the routine on its predetermined course. Aside from his characterization of Dud, Dudley would play a variety of idiotic, incompetent characters. Moore was also amazing for his ability to improvise, never missing a chance to ad-lib if he thought the opportunity was right.

Moore exuded the moods and traits of the comedians he adulated in his performances, without ever consciously acknowledging it. He was capable of any style of humor, and combined the physical agility of Peter Sellers, the infectious laugh of Stan Laurel, the pantomimic skills of Marcel Marceau, and the witty verbal gyrations of Terry-Thomas. Moore has mentioned in numerous interviews that although he never had any major comedy influences as a child, he did have his favorites: "I've loved all sorts of comedians over the years. Fernandel is someone I loved when I was a kid. Marcel Marceau, Peter Sellers, especially in his early films, although I would watch him any time. I was very influenced by his radio shows when I was a kid: *The Goon Show, Take It From Here,* and *Ray's A Laugh.* In film, I love Terry-Thomas. But I think every comedian I've ever seen, I enjoyed to some extent."

Dudley became anxious to show off his talents to film producers, and before long, Cook and Moore found their opportunity. Film producer-and-director Bryan Forbes was filming a comedy spoof based on the Robert Louis Stevenson/Lloyd Osbourne tale, THE WRONG BOX, when he enlisted Cook and Moore to play the roles of two greedy nephews, Morris (Peter) and John (Dudley). Unfortunately, Dudley's introduction into the tricky world of film-making was not made smoothly nor easily.

According to Dudley, Forbes wasn't from the stock of directors who felt secure relying upon the comic instincts of his comedians when enacting a scripted scene. He instead preferred wild camera mugging, exaggerated gags, and heavy-handed slapstick to generate laughter. Dudley was very dissatisfied with having his comic hands tied and grew tired of his offbeat style of direction, and of the overall attitude of the director himself towards comedy. Expressing his displeasure, Moore said, "I never found what Bryan did very easy to follow. It was like aping movements and facial expressions, even though it wasn't constantly like that. He gave you very little room to do your own thing." Although Moore was less than supportive of Forbes' method, critics stood almost unanimously behind the director when *THE WRONG BOX* made its world premiere in New York on July 19, 1966. A majority of film critics remarked that it was Forbes' direction, in fact, that was primarily responsible for making *THE WRONG BOX* a surprise comedy masterpiece.

In a story shaped around greed and mistaken identity, two elderly brothers, Masterman (John Mills) and Joseph Finsburg (Ralph Richardson), are bound together in a tontine, a financial arrangement in which the last surviving family member stands to inherit the large remaining fortune. The film revolves around the scheming of the brothers and their attempts to kill each other in order to gain the inheritance. At one point in the film, Joseph plots to bump off dear old Masterman, so that he might pass on the inheritance to his grandson, Michael (Michael Caine). Yet every attempt to have done with his brother fails, while two money-hungry nephews, Morris and John, begin hatching plans of their own. Needless to say, they too have their eyes on the inheritance, which would make them the richest men in all of England.

As the plot thickens, Morris and John

erroneously believe that Masterman is dead, (the result of a previous murder attempt that didn't work), and that Uncle Joseph Finsburg has died in a tragic train wreck. Confident that the inheritance is now theirs, the devious duo convince Joseph's physician to sign a death certificate, thereby making Joseph's death official and enabling them to collect the cash. With the money firmly in hand, Morris and John attempt to stash the loot in a safe hiding place, for which they are subsequently arrested due to their very suspicious appearances. After the villainous cousins are exposed, Joseph and Masterman (who was also assumed dead), decide to award the entire inheritance to Michael and Julia, Joseph's ward, who have fallen in love, and they live happily ever.

The funniest episode of the entire film is, perhaps, the frantic chase that erupts after cousins Cook and Moore recover the elusive inheritance. Peter and Dudley pack the filthy money into a coffin, deposit it in the back of a horse-drawn hearse, and gallop off to safety. Not far behind, however, are Michael and his sweetheart, who borrow a hearse of their own and set out in hot pursuit. The chase turns into a madcap romp through the streets of London, into a park where a band concert is in progress, and onward to the most likely destination, a local cemetery, where Cook and Moore try burying "the wrong box" (a substitute coffin) to fool Michael and Julie into believing that the money is in the cemetery plot.

THE WRONG BOX is British comedy at its best, mostly due to Cook and Moore, who grace the screen with their special brand of tomfoolery and unadulterated lunacy. Michael Caine contributes an impressive comedy performance, while Peter Sellers is delightful in a cameo role. Forbes' direction seems crisp and razor-sharp in delivering the necessary comic punch and not nearly as for-

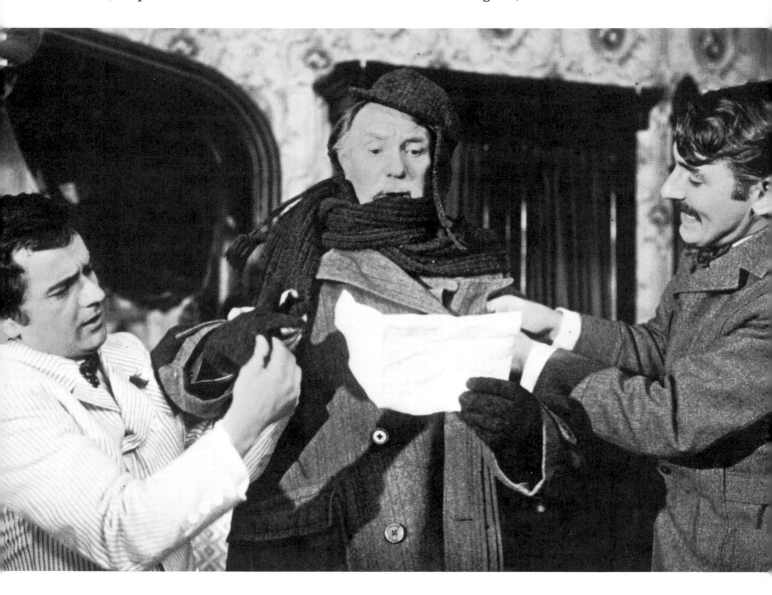

mula-oriented as Moore has intimated. *THE WRONG BOX*, which has since evolved into a minor cult classic, is undoubtedly one of the most cleverly designed film satires to come out of England in recent years.

Critics were in agreement over the film's merit, as exemplified by Judith Crist, who wrote: "*THE WRONG BOX* is the right movie, an irresistibly delicious delight. Top talent, romance, high-comedy, and hysteria." *NEWSWEEK* said: "*THE WRONG BOX* is as funny, sunny and urbane a movie as any audience could ask for." *TIME* maga-

zine added: "The vogue sick screen comedy has obviously fallen into capable hands. Softened by the ruddy glow of the gaslight era, *THE WRONG BOX* makes graveside humor a gas." Peculiarly, British film critics were not so kind, however, finding many flaws in the movie. A *TIMES* of London critic blasted: "The film Bryan Forbes has made out of it (the original story) is so far from the original that questions of fidelity and betrayal hardly seem applicable." While Forbes received most of the praise, some critics recognized Cook and Moore's side-splitting antics for the show-stealers they were, as a pair of "craven city cousins." But *THE WRONG BOX*, produced at just under $2 million, bombed at the box office despite the generally favorable reviews. Critics were unable to understand why the film failed, but American filmgoers knew all too well—they had difficulty catching on to the British humor.

Since *THE WRONG BOX* was having trouble attracting viewers, Cook and Moore decided that they would turn their noses away from film-making for a while. Rather than undertake any new film projects, they instead turned to the music business and recorded their first single, *"LS Bumblebee"* on January 27, 1967. The song was originally composed by former Beatle John Lennon and intended for the Beatles' new album, *Sgt. Pepper's Lonely Hearts Club Band*, marketed around the same time as *"Bumblebee."* Instead, John offered the song to Cook and Moore, both of whom he met when doing a guest spot on an episode of their former BBC television series, *NOT ONLY . . . BUT ALSO.*

"LS Bumblebee" spoofed the whole psychedelic song craze which was so prevalent at the time, and capitalized upon the heavy metal sound and space-oriented lyrics associated with these songs. On side two of this unique single, Cook and Moore harmonize together on *"Bee Side,"* their duets sounding for all the world like the Beatles themselves! While the record inspired moderate sales, *"LS Bumblebee"* failed to win over the hearts of music critics, and became Cook and Moore's first musical recording disappointment, obviously putting a crimp in their hopes of musical advancement. But two months later the Screen Writers Guild of Great Britain heralded Cook and Moore at its annual awards dinner for the team's once-popular BBC television series, *NOT ONLY*

. . . BUT ALSO, by awarding the duo an award for writing the Best Light Entertainment series. It became one of many such honors that they would receive in the ensuing years.

After taking some time to savor their new status, Cook and Moore began work on their next comedy film romp, *BEDAZZLED*, for which Cook and Moore wrote the screenplay (Dudley penned the music as well). They also starred in the title roles, and enlisted the aid of Stanley Donen to produce and direct. Donen was already renowned throughout the cinema world for such prize-winning film achievements as MGM's classic musical, *SINGIN' IN THE RAIN*, and the 1957 screen version of *FUNNY FACE* with Audrey Hepburn and Fred Astaire. The British film-maker was producing *BEDAZZLED* under his own company banner, Stanley Donen Productions, and releasing the film through 20th Century-Fox. Incidentally, for trivia lovers, one of the film's co-stars was none other than the young and utterly enchanting actress, Raquel Welch.

BEDAZZLED premiered internationally on December 10, 1967, during a movie season which film executives were calling "full of surprises." *BEDAZZLED* was released at the time when Dustin Hoffman was in the midst of winning enormous critical acclaim for his performance in *THE GRADUATE*, while Richard Harris and Vanessa Redgrave were capturing the hearts and minds of romantics everywhere in the epic, *CAMELOT*. Even Charlton Heston was up to his old miraculous tricks in the film reissue of Cecil B. DeMille's *THE TEN COMMANDMENTS*. So where did an innocent, low-budget foreign comedy like *BEDAZZLED* fit in? It didn't. In the 1967 film season, a year bursting with hit after hit, *BEDAZZLED* was an undisputed miss.

Even by today's standards, *BE-*

DAZZLED (which could have been more aptly titled, *BEDEVILED*), ranks among one of Cook and Moore's strangest contributions to the realm of comedy cinema. The story reprises the timeworn theme of a man who sells his soul to the Devil, this time in exchange for seven wishes. Cook and Moore slightly modify the old tale by casting Dudley as Stanley Moon, a restaurant short order cook who has absolutely no confidence when it comes to wooing women. Cook, as Mr. George Spiggot, alias The Devil, calls upon Moon to offer him the chance to fulfill all of his dreams by signing over his soul. Moon—tragically undersexed, meek and feeble-minded—agrees, provided the Devil will grant him seven wishes *and* will help him to win the love of Margaret (Eleanor Bron), a

waitress in the restaurant where he works. He lands Margaret all right, but his passions overcome him and he discovers that the Devil has more control over him than he realizes. With each granted wish, Moon meets up with members of the Devil's evil committee, who try to sway him to their point of view. The members of this comitteee are Lillian Lust (Raquel Welch); Vanity (Alba); Mr. Anger (Robert Russell); Mr. Envy (Barry Humphries); Mr. Gluttony (Parnell Mc-Garry); Mr. Sloth (Howard Gooney); and Ms. Avarice (Daniele Noel). For the fulfillment of Moon's final wish, the Devil sends the unfortunate man off, with his adorable Margaret in tow, to a bizarre convent, where, dressed as nuns, the two are forced to bounce indefinitely on trampolines!

Dudley Moore and John Lennon in an episode of "Not Only . . . But Also," 1967.

Dudley Moore as Stanley Moon and Raquel Welch as Lust in a scene from "Bedazzled," 1967.

unable to imbue the script with the consistency it so desperately needed. BEDAZZLED was only fairly successful as comic satire, trying too hard to be funny, and failing to exploit the rich talents of Cook and Moore.

Moore is fond of this film, because it marks his first starring role and is, in part, autobiographical in content. Furthermore, Stanley Moon's uneven life of ups and downs resembles Dudley's own career—at the pinnacle of success one day, nearly nonexistent at the box office the next. Moon's character seems a bit like the real Dudley; his ineptitude when approaching those of the opposite sex, and his constant bouts with feelings of rejection, all point towards personality similarities. In the film, Stanley Moon attributes his own shortcomings and his inability to subdue members of the opposite sex to a basic lack of confidence, not to mention his abbreviated stature. (Dudley remarked during the making of this film that he felt inferior when it came to dating taller women.) Although Dudley was very much a sex symbol to his predominantly female fans, Moon's plump, dumpy physique seemed hardly the kind of super-macho image that women found sexy. His cropped, untidy hair, greased behind the tops of his ears, added to his somewhat slovenly appearance and unattractiveness.

Whatever affinity Dudley might feel for the film, however, *BEDAZZLED* fell short of being the successful film he had hoped it would be, and it continued to receive chilly reviews. *TIME* magazine cited the film as a technical disaster, maintaining that the script was at fault: "Actor-writers Cook and Moore, who once were half of the wily foursome in *BEYOND THE FRINGE*, have failed to grasp the basic difference between a four-minute skit and a 107-minute movie." *LOS ANGELES TIMES* critic Charles Champlin denounced the comedy as "the most infuriating picture seen all year—

BEDAZZLED is a simple farce, modestly portrayed, sometimes tastelessly sacrilegious, yet through it all, mildly amusing. The story experiences problems with its continuity towards the end of the production, since the film is essentially a sketch stretched out to feature-film length. Stanley Donen's direction is free from restraint, though he was infuriating because the best of it is so deliciously inventively good and the worst of it so appallingly distastefully awful." *NEWSWEEK*, on the other hand, enjoyed the film, calling it "a fluffy and funny version of the Faust legend in mod dress."

In an interview, Dudley admitted that he felt *BEDAZZLED* got the lukewarm reception it did chiefly because it was so different from anything he and Cook had attempted since their BBC television series. And with so many startling changes disrupting people's lives during the late 1960s, perhaps audiences sought familiar faces and acts in the safe, fantasy world of the movies. Unfortunately, the old reliable styles of Cook and Moore were not to be found in *BEDAZZLED.*

Dudley's career could not afford another box office flop. His climb up the ladder of success fluctuated as often as the stock exchange rate on Wall Street. And like stocks and bonds that have not yet matured, what Moore needed more than ever was an impetus to help his career meet with his own expectations. The first step was to temporarily abandon his association with Peter Cook. Originally, Cook and Moore's next film assignment was to be *THE WHACK*, a musical comedy (also under the direction of Stanley Donen) starring the duo as a pair of wacky doctors. But with *BEDAZZLED* drawing a great deal of criticism and doing poorly at the box office, Donen changed his mind about beginning the project. So did Moore. Dudley pursued solo ventures for a while, hoping to mend the wounds of his film misadventures.

Moore now began writing his first movie screenplay, called *30 IS A DANGEROUS AGE, CYNTHIA* (two other writers were added later, Joseph McGrath and John Wells). In the film, Moore plays an obscure musician trying to carve his niche by composing a successful musical before reaching the age of thirty. The script captured the interest of former Beatles' film producer, Walter Shenson, who financed the picture for a million dollars through his own production firm. Moore, anxious to get started, recommended that Shenson hire film-maker Joseph McGrath to direct this lighthearted

Moore as short-order cook Stanley Moon in "Bedazzled," 1967.

comedy-musical-fantasy. McGrath and Moore's paths apparently crossed once before when McGrath piloted the young comedian in his hit BBC television series, *NOT ONLY... BUT ALSO.*

Dudley's ideas for the original screenplay were derived from actual incidents in his life. His girl friend, Suzy Kendall, was cast in the role of an artist born in Belper, Derbyshire (Kendall was born in Belper, believe it or not, and was at one time an artist herself). Dudley has also admitted since to sharing an obsession with the film's hero Rupert Street, to compose an *opera* before *his* thirtieth birthday. Even Moore's mother, Ada, had something to do with the film. "My mother should get some credit," Dudley says. "She always sent me my laundry through the mail—just like Rupert's does in the film. And like Rupert's, she always included a sack of lemon drops and some bread pudding in the package."

Dudley was comfortable with his new screen role, but problems arose. Moore has remarked that he didn't approve of the many changes that were made in the original draft of his screenplay. "After three-quarters of an hour, the film took a direction that I didn't want it to take—there were too many cooks in that one," Moore says. "I really wanted it to be a simple story about a man who wants to compose music. I didn't have a girl in it, or the fact that he wants to get married. That seemed to me, irrelevant."

Dudley's misgivings about the film were unfortunate, since the role of Rupert Street seemed perfectly engineered to display his myriad talents as actor, comedian, and musician. The plot presents the ambitious Street, his project hindered by two main obstacles —money to finance his musical revue and confidence in himself. His job playing piano at a Scottish nightclub doesn't help either— saddled with the task of entertaining the local audiences, Rupert hardly ever has time to compose his musical extravaganza. Soon, however, two events change his life: meeting and falling in love with an art student, Louise Hammond (Suzy Kendall), and forming a fruitful partnership with an old vaudevillian (Eddie Foy, Jr.) who helps Rupert to produce the idealistic musical.

It is at this point, when the antics so well-known to Dudley's films are expected to begin, that the film actually starts to unravel. True, Rupert does manage to produce his musical and win the heart of his lover, and after facing considerable adversity. But Dudley's comedic sense is never knee-slappingly hilarious. Instead he seems to have emphasized the theatrical and musical aspects of his endeavor. And Dudley may have been right when he said the love interest between his character and Kendall's young artist derailed the meaning he had hoped for in the film. Though Kendall's charm and sex appeal are pleasant additions to the film, her character is not vital to the plot. It would have been clearly acceptable if the film had ended on the high note of Moore producing his musical. The marriage between Dudley and Kendall does nothing to enhance the film's ending, and seems a bit predictable.

Nevertheless there are successful comic bits that showcase Dudley's perpetually sharp form. For example, Moore attempts to seduce Kendall with a ballad sung in the manner of Noel Coward, during which he mimics Bach, Beethoven, Mozart, and Handel, with rib-tickling results. When he and Kendall finally consummate their blossoming friendship, Dudley imagines himself the equal of such screen lovers as Rudolph Valentino and Douglas Fairbanks, Sr. Perhaps the best sequences in the film are his nightclub piano performances—during one number Moore suddenly bursts into a hysterical StepinFetchit/Negro dialect, while comically pounding on the ivory keys of the piano.

But as a whole (and while Moore might disagree), *30 IS A DANGEROUS AGE, CYNTHIA* will probably be looked upon in years to come as a minor musical-comedy achievement. Though Dudley's performance added grace to the production, Suzy Kendall was sexy, genuinely attractive and convincing as Moore's oversexed girl next door, and Eddie Foy, Jr. returned to the screen in a film role naturally suited for his type, the many competent performances given by these screen semi-veterans could not make the film a blockbuster. The director, Joseph McGrath, was adept with his use of the camera and the rather thin script, but *30 IS A DANGEROUS AGE, CYNTHIA* will surely rank as Moore's least remembered movie, as the critics seemed to agree when the film opened in New York on March 4, 1968.

HOLLYWOOD REPORTER critic John Mahoney declared that the film "suffers from the precocity of Dudley Moore, as well as a script and direction which takes no aim but leaves no target untouched. 'CYNTHIA' is fun, though, clearly less so for its audience than its makers." Charles Champlin of the *LOS ANGELES TIMES* commented: "The weaknesses include a certain infirmity of purpose in which the individual moments seem more than ever like revue sketches hung on the amusing cobwebs of continuity." The *MOTION PICTURE HERALD*, a leading Hollywood trade paper, was one of the few publications to vote in favor of Moore's film and performance. It said that *CYNTHIA* would "sell filmgoers on Moore's reputation as a comic and satirist." In the United Kingdom, *TIMES* of London critic John Russell Taylor wrote that the film gives the impression of "being made up as they go along." He added that the film lacked discipline in its construction and execution of gags: "To a con-siderable extent this vehicle for Dudley Moore stands or falls on how far you go for him. I quite like his music, but fail to find him very funny."

Along with the generally poor reviews, Columbia Pictures, which released *30 IS A DANGEROUS AGE, CYNTHIA*, badly mishandled the promotion of the film. For uncertain reasons, the British-made comedy was publicized in connection with the mini-skirt generation, the Beatles, and the Sexual Revolution, when in actuality the film had very little to do with these themes at all. The theatre ads were misleading, and since foreign films are generally harder to sell to an American audience, Columbia Pictures decided that the more racy angle would bring larger numbers of filmgoers to the theatre. They soon found out, however, that this strategy did not help box-office sales one iota, because miniskirts soon faded as quietly from the scene as *30 IS A DANGEROUS AGE, CYNTHIA* did from local theater screens.

While fashion designers were trying to brainstorm a successor to the miniskirt, Dudley was also searching for a change, the kind that wouldn't impede the growth of his career. Moore was now in limbo for the first time since the completion of *BEYOND THE FRINGE*. His solo film debut with *30 IS A DANGEROUS AGE, CYNTHIA*, weighed heavily upon his mind. Moore felt that he had failed to meet his personal goals with the project, and was troubled by the inconsistencies of his career. To smooth the rougher edges of this problem, he made a brief appearance on a BBC television special, *GOOD-BYE AGAIN*, but this performance did not accomplish much more than the satisfaction of United Kingdom fans. The problem of no new incoming offers remained for Dudley on both sides of the Atlantic Ocean.

One aspect of the *CYNTHIA...* story

did come true: his marriage to Suzy Kendall. Following their three year courtship, Dudley and Suzy were wed without fanfare on June 14, 1968 at the Hampstead Register Office in a private ceremony. The wedding was kept secret from all but two close friends, one of whom was Peter Cook. Moore's own secretary, Diana Borghys, remarked that even she was unaware of the marriage until after the ceremonies were over. As she recalled, "I had no idea they were getting married until Suzy phoned me to say that it had happened." The two were not interested in staging a lavish church wedding with hundreds of guests. Suzy preferred a private ceremony for this, her second marriage. Dudley was confident

that his marriage to Kendall would succeed, secure in the knowledge that she was right for him after three years of life together.

With the added responsibility of marriage now on his shoulders, Moore tried to determine what his next move should be. He occasionally collaborated with Peter Cook on a number of different project ideas, but formed nothing concrete. In fact, they did not work together again professionally until film producer Ken Annakin signed them to appear in his forthcoming film, *THOSE DARING YOUNG MEN IN THEIR JAUNTY JALOPIES* (also known as *MONTE CARLO OR BUST*).

Unlike their previous film productions

right, **Cook and Moore as a pair of capricious Coppers in "The Bed Sitting Room," 1969.**

left, **Cook and Moore looking dusty and disappointed in "Those Daring Young Men in Their Jaunty Jalopies," 1969.**

together, Cook and Moore were not given large parts in *THOSE DARING YOUNG MEN IN THEIR JAUNTY JALOPIES*, a sequel to *THE GREAT RACE* (another film based on an international race car competition). In this action-packed comedy, Dudley and Peter were participants in a late 1920s Monte Carlo Rally. Their adversaries in the comic adventure included Terry-Thomas, Tony Curtis, Susan Hampshire, Gert Frobe, and two frenzied Italian comedians, Walter Chiari and Lando Buzzanca. Cook and Moore made it to the finish line, which was more than the other competitors could claim, their faces charred by the explosive remnants of their souped-up race car. There was no

question that this film included one of their finest performances together, and consequently, the entire film was a hit. *THOSE DARING YOUNG MEN IN THEIR JAUNTY JALOPIES* made its world premiere at New York's Astor Theatre on May 29, 1969 to critical accolades and healthy box-office returns.

This latest triumph afforded Cook and Moore with the happy realization that film-goers wanted to see much more of them on the silver screen. In order to appease the appetites of their fans, the two quickly agreed to appear in filmmaker Richard Lester's black comedy, *THE BED SITTING ROOM*, which was adapted from the anti-war play by Spike

Milligan and John Antrobus.

According to Moore, THE BED SITTING ROOM lacked thematic direction, with many problems stemming from Dick Lester's direction. As Dudley tells it: "Dick Lester never seemed to know what he wanted. He gave peculiar instructions, which were hard to follow. He wanted different opinions but rejected them all, which was very disconcerting."

These technical flaws were apparent when THE BED SITTING ROOM was finally issued for world-wide public consumption on September 28, 1969, premiering in New York. Initially, critics did not seem to know what to make of the farce. Clearly, Dudley was correct in his assessment of the story and characters; they did indeed appear to take a backseat to the indecisive direction of Lester, whose previous film credits (the Beatles' A HARD DAY'S NIGHT for one) were much more appealing and sharply executed.

Designed to take a farcical look at the modern problems of the loss of values and contemporary morality, THE BED SITTING ROOM takes place three years after the cessation of the shortest nuclear war in history (2 minutes, 28 seconds). Located in London, twenty survivors rummage through the endless amounts of rubble, which at one time had been their beloved city.

This British-produced blackest of comedies satirizes the horror and devastation of nuclear war to emphasize its pacifistic statement. Each vignette focuses on the attempts of the wounded survivors to overcome the physical mutations that arise as they are affected by the creeping radiation. Among the wandering souls who weather the nuclear storm are Lord Fortnum (Ralph Richardson), who is in the process of turning into a bed-sitting room; Penelope (Rita Tushingham), 17-months pregnant and still awaiting delivery; her overzealous Mum (Mona Wash-bourne) and her Dad (Arthur Loew), who are also slowly mutating—one into a cupboard and the other into a parrot (which is eventually cooked and eaten).

The cast of survivors also includes Captain Bules Martin (Michael Hordern), posing as a roving BBC reporter, who takes Penelope's hand in marriage, only to become the father of a mutant beast child (resulting from the side-effects of nuclear radiation). Completing the cast are Alan (Richard Warwick), Penelope's first love, whom she marries when Martin no longer proves sexually capable (Penelope eventually bears a normal child who saves the kingdom from another nuclear bombardment); and the moronic policemen (Dudley Moore and Peter Cook), who hover over the survivors in their broken down Volkswagen suspended from the end of a helium balloon. Dudley also mutates into, of all things, a dog,

Despite sporadic attempts at surrealism and inventiveness, THE BED SITTING ROOM is not inherently funny. Certainly, the tragic effects of nuclear war provide filmgoers with food for thought, but the subject matter cannot be chuckled over. The treatment is too morbid, too unrelentingly downbeat, even to qualify as black comedy.

Director Lester's blackout style of direction comes across as too methodical, losing the audience as the film wanders aimlessly along. A sketch about nuclear war has comedic possibilities if treated succinctly, but for a ninety-minute film, there was not enough material. (DR. STRANGELOVE succeeded, however, where THE BED SITTING ROOM failed, due to an emphasis on the perpetrators of the holocaust, rather than the pitiable victims.) This film, despite its social commentary, makes clear a different point; though the film possessed many good qualities, time and talent are wasted without strong scripting. Additionally, Cook and Moore were assigned even smaller roles in *THE BED SIT-TING ROOM* than they had received in *THOSE DARING YOUNG MEN IN THEIR JAUNTY JALOPIES.*

Again, critics were quick to pounce upon the faults of this revolutionary comedy when it burst upon theatre screens worldwide. The *NEW YORKER* magazine was clearly offended by the film, commenting "One laughs from time to time, but, as in so much modern English far-out satire, there's no spirit, no rage, nothing left but ghastly incessant sinking-island humor." A critic for *DAILY VARIETY*, Hollywood's major trade paper hotline, took a similar position on the film's shortcomings, stating "...a film of nonsense and characters who remain alien to laughter." Critic James Robert Parish of the *MOTION PICTURE HERALD* felt the film deserved a poor rating, adding that its "occasional bits of slight humor and wit fail to convey much new insight into the prejudice of society."

With *THE BED SITTING ROOM* not faring well critically—marking Dudley's second film catastrophe in one year, Moore began to expand his horizons beyond the realm of movies. Soon he was writing songs for other film productions and looking into potentially challenging avenues.

Filmmaking wasn't working out the way he'd planned, and the possibility of a flourishing film career seemed doubtful. Moore again turned to music as a viable and satisfying option, and composed a number of popular musical scores for such films as *INADMISSIBLE EVIDENCE* (1968)—a theme he also sings— and *STAIRCASE* (1969). Dudley was caught in a tantalizing, frustrating cycle of success and setback, with a combination of poor judgment and bad luck contributing to the unevenness of his career. Chances were that as Dudley matured as a performer, he would begin to have a string of successes.

Dudley Moore as yet another character from "Not Only . . . But Also," 1970.

CHAPTER 4

"Dudley Plays It Again"

The year 1969 was a turbulent season of experimentation and expansion for Dudley. Romantically, his marriage to Suzy Kendall was floundering, and professionally, he was unsure of which route to take, so he channeled his energies into many show business ventures. During this year Moore composed scores, presented stage productions, and recorded a number of jazz LPs, with the hope that his career would finally coalesce. Dudley was keenly aware that he needed a definite direction, and in order to discover what that direction might be, kept a hand in many areas.

Moore was dissatisfied with the film roles he had undertaken in the past. He felt his appearances were not much more than one-dimensional cameos, and yearned for meatier, more challenging roles that would allow him to grow as an actor. Only two of his film portrayals, Stanley Moon of BE-DAZZLED and Rupert Street of 30 IS A DANGEROUS AGE, CYNTHIA, provided Moore with an adequate amount of screen time in which to showcase his diversity of talents. But to Dudley's dismay, timely comedy roles seemed in short supply and were being awarded to other actors. His only choice appeared to be handling the matter himself.

Consequently, Moore returned to the London stage with his own adaptation of the Woody Allen play, PLAY IT AGAIN, SAM, which premiered at the Globe Theater in London on September 11, 1969. While critics gave the show mixed reviews, theatregoers turned out in droves to applaud Moore's comic performance. Dudley received many respectable notices, but critics complained that he did not quite catch Woody Allen's "personification of neurotic, failurehaunted, urban Jewish-American manhood gone to seed."

In Dudley's opinion, the play's comic intention was to contrast sex in the movies with sex in reality. To emphasize this point he anglicized the text and altered many of the jokes, while attempting to retain "that peculiarly Jewish comic gloom" characteristic of Allen's work. But some critics did not think the changes that Dudley had made were successful. As TIMES of London drama critic Irving Wardle wrote: "Padded out to just over two hours with the aid of two intervals and a late curtain, this show may scrape home simply on the combined appeal of Dudley Moore (minus piano) and eight appetizing girls. Otherwise it supplies yet another instance of the folly of trying to anglicize American comedy..."

PLAY IT AGAIN, SAM centers around the trials and tribulations of Allan Felix (Dudley), a young film critic in New York City struggling to revive his self respect and sex life, not necessarily in that order. After a demoralizing divorce, Felix relies largely on his best friends, Dick and Linda Christie, to arrange dates for him because his confidence in matters of the heart has been shattered. As he clumsily attempts to seduce the nubile sexy females he encounters, Felix conjures up the spirit of Humphrey Bogart, one of Hollywood's greatest lady-killers, as an inspirational presence and role model. The character's vain attempts to emulate Bogie's dashing lovemaking techniques result in repeated disappointments, although Felix does, towards the conclusion of the play, enjoy a brief affair with the girl of his dreams.

Moore's performance was rich with comic pathos, in accordance with his character, who, though successful in the business world, is nonetheless dissatisfied with the fickle nature of romance. The theme of the play stresses Felix's search for his true emotions and identity, and his realization that he is more acceptable to women as himself rather than as an unconvincing impersonation of Humphrey Bogart.

Ironically, at the same time he was playing the character of a newly divorced Allan Felix, Dudley began experiencing his first marital woes with Suzy Kendall. During interviews he confessed that he had been influenced by his private life as he prepared for the role, and this was what gave his performance a deeper sense of raw emotion. With his marriage on the verge of breaking up, and his many insecurities regarding his career development, Dudley was again in need of a change.

So when the final curtain closed on *PLAY IT AGAIN, SAM*, Moore and his old friend Peter Cook accepted a new offer to star in a third season of their BBC television series, *NOT ONLY . . . BUT ALSO*, slated to be aired during the spring of 1970. The teaming of Peter Cook and Dudley Moore was just as fresh, and the humor as unabating as it had been when the show was new to viewers.

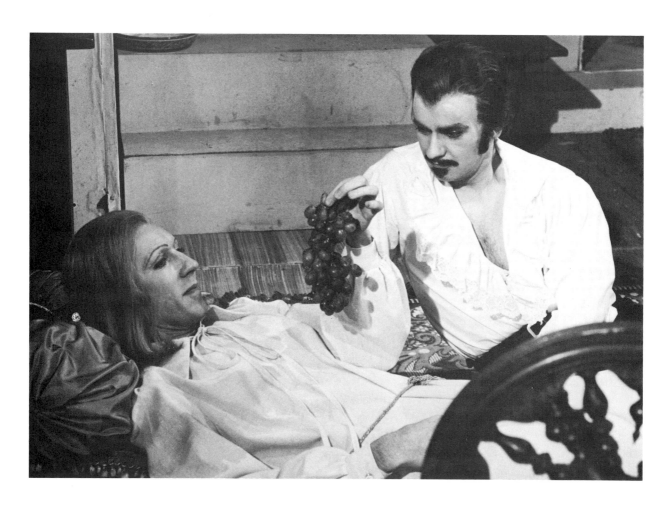

Peter Cook as a rather dubious Greta Garbo and Dudley Moore as a pint-sized John Barrymore from "Not Only . . . But Also," 1970.

The first episode featured one Pete and Dud sketch with Moore and Cook reminiscing over their public school years, followed by a parody of a television program on the life of Greta Garbo. Former *GOON SHOW* member Spike Milligan also guest-starred. (The "Goons" were a well-known team of English comic actors, with the most notable among them being Peter Sellers.)

When the show was discontinued, Dudley and Peter moved on to their next project, to write and star in *GOOD EVENING*, a stage production which was being touted as the successor to the ever-popular *BEYOND THE FRINGE*. It was in *GOOD EVENING*, that, for the very first time, Cook and Moore received top billing as a team.

Before beginning *GOOD EVENING*, however, Cook and Moore each purchased handsome new homes in London. Moore's dwelling was located in Islington, while Cook feathered his nest in Hampstead, the area where Dudley and Suzy had lived during the early portion of their marriage. Moore had decided to relocate because his two year marriage to Suzy Kendall had fallen apart and she was filing for divorce. The marriage had produced no children, and no reasons were given for the separation other than that their relationship had become strained. Dudley later confessed his share of the blame for contributing to the disintegration of their marriage, citing as causes his acts of silence and the difficulties he had expressing his feelings. It was the second divorce for the 30-year-old Kendall and Moore's first.

Dudley now addressed all of his attention to the success of *GOOD EVENING*, (initially entitled *BEHIND THE FRIDGE* but changed to avoid a mix-up with "Beyond the Fringe") which opened as part of a 1971 tour of Australia and New Zealand. Dudley has credited the show's five-month engagement

"GOOD EVENING"

in Australia with furnishing the extra time that he and Peter needed to tighten, prune, and arrange the revue according to the reception of each skit. Happily for Cook and Moore, they found they still enjoyed performing before a live audience as much as they had twelve years earlier in *BEYOND THE FRINGE*. As Moore recalled, "When we were in Australia with this show, there were nights when I couldn't think of anything being more enjoyable. It was such tremendous fun, and you came off absolutely ecstatic and jumping about the place. In New Zealand, it really hit a ridiculous pitch of enjoyment in performance. It was marvelous."

The show traveled to London, where it played for almost a year (beginning on No-

45

vember 21, 1972 at Cambridge Hall) before moving on to New York's Plymouth Theatre on November 14, 1973. Of the London stage version, critic Irving Wardle of the *TIMES* wrote: "Fans will need no encouragement to see the pair in action—the show certainly sets one up at the outpost of original and intelligent fun..."

Prior to the show's Manhattan debut, Moore spoke with reporters about the impossibility of giving "an ideal performance" on opening night, with three hundred financial backers upfront worrying about their investment. "That edge of nervousness is not only in the performer, it's in the audience," Dudley exclaimed backstage. Despite Moore's trepidation, critics lauded the show as "the surprise hit of the year," and Cook and Moore went on to win the coveted Tony awards for their dazzling performances. The *LOS ANGELES TIMES* hailed Cook and Moore as "both talented and skilled—with Moore having the edge on wryness, and Cook, also known to kick up his heels, for displaying a uniquely British deadpan." The stage show ran for almost four consecutive years before making its only limited run at the Los Angeles Shubert Theatre from July 23, 1975 to August 31, 1975.

In spite of the name change, *GOOD EVENING* was similar to *BEYOND THE FRINGE*—not surprising since Cook and Moore, though 12 years older, were no less impish or irreverent. The humor was again a typically British diet of mugging, pithy dialogue, and hilarious sight gags. Even more importantly, Cook and Moore's self-esteem received a significant boost because *GOOD EVENING* demonstrated just how far the duo had come since their days as stars of *BEYOND THE FRINGE*. They not only excelled in their performances but were much more polished and self-assured, with an even greater ability to coax laughter from an audience.

GOOD EVENING was composed of fifteen numbers, three of which were piano pieces played by Moore. In the opening sketch, aptly titled "Hello," Moore and Cook portray two men who meet on the street and, as old friends who haven't seen each other in a long time are wont to do, express the sincerest interest in each other's children, wives, jobs, reminisce about old friends, and bask in the fun of bumping into an almost-forgotten acquaintance. The only quirk here is that in reality the two have never actually met before... they are complete strangers.

In another popular sketch, Moore and his son discuss the untimely death of their

Pete and Dudley in the BBC-television version of "Good Evening," in 1973.

46

wife and mother in a hospital. The end, it seems, came in a Rube Goldberg-like chain reaction that took the lives of 897 other patients! The tragedy started when a shriek of pain by Mom caused her false teeth to pop out of her mouth and shatter a light bulb hanging from the ceiling. A nurse then slipped on the broken glass, knocking another nurse out of the window into the path of a passing car which killed her and went on to demolish the entire hospital building. As Dudley concluded, "Suffice it to say, I was the sole survivor."

Cook and Moore followed that skit with one of the fabled sketches from *BEYOND THE FRINGE*, "One Leg Too Few," featuring Dudley as Mr. Spiggot, the one-legged Tarzan hopeful, and then "Crime and Punishment," in which Dudley, cast as a schoolmaster, attempts to administer the rod to a pupil (Peter Cook) who happens to be *twice* his size. Cook's crime? Swiping some gym shoes from the gym teacher's locker, for which he is supposed to receive a lashing from Moore, the principal. But as the much-taller-than-life student warns, "If you lay a finger on me, I'll smash your stupid little face in." Dudley takes heed and then makes a peace offering, some items from his own stash of goodies—a pornographic magazine, some money, and preferred treatment in the future. In "The Frog and Peach," Moore hosts a television talk show with his guest, the owner of a restaurant, situated in a bog, that serves only *two* entrees—frogs and peaches! During the interview, the owner

Cook and Moore from their controversial "Gospel Truth" sketch in "Good Evening," 1972.

(Peter Cook) explains the evolution of the offbeat menu: "The idea came to me in the bath— a great number of things come to me in the bath, mainly mosquitoes, various forms of water snakes, but on this occasion, a rather stunning and unique idea." Cook adds that business was mind-boggling for some time, but then, "Business hasn't been and there hasn't been any business."

The show's most controversial skit was entitled "Gospel Truth," and featured Moore as a reporter for the *BETHLEHEM STAR* coming to interview Mr. Arthur Shepherd (Cook), who claims to have witnessed the birth of Jesus Christ. His motto: "Shepherd by name, shepherd by nature." The sketch ran the gamut of Biblical and Holy Land comedy.

GOOD EVENING was the professional kind of British comedy revue that did justice to Moore's considerable talents. His music, improvisations, comic nuances and precise timing were all finely tuned and kept the audience in thrall. It came as no surprise that film and television producers began to take a closer look at Dudley.

Dudley had also brought organization and a renewed enthusiasm to his working relationship with Peter Cook, which he credits for the success of *GOOD EVENING*. According to Moore, the only serious disagreement of their 16-year association came during their *GOOD EVENING* tour in Australia, when Peter couldn't resist sampling Australian wine one night before the show. Cook's tipsy demeanor caused him to flub some lines during the performance, completely unnerving Moore and jeopardizing the future of their partnership. Their differences were quickly reconciled, however, and from them emerged a deep respect between the partners that served to make them more candid with each other. Their working relationship was actually

quite extraordinary, especially since Moore has claimed that they "were diametrically opposed in everything." For instance, Cook took great delight in smoking and drinking while Moore did not. Peter enjoyed discussing politics, while Dudley was happy to ruminate over his intimate experiences with other women. How did theirs remain a successful partnership?

Moore once explained: "Enjoyment, enthusiasm, being amused by each other. I make him laugh a great deal and he makes me. When we work together, you can see the enjoyment in our eyes. There was no lack of concentration—there was total devotion. We listen to each other and react to each other. It's a total involvement in what we are doing—and enthusiasm that makes it happen."

Moore believes that their mutual dedication was responsible for enabling them to perform so cohesively together and to collaborate jointly on many creative writing projects. Brilliant comedy routines do not simply appear in dreams or drunken visions. There must be, as the saying follows, a method to the madness. To write the sketches for *GOOD EVENING,* Cook and Moore would brainstorm with a tape recorder nearby, then edit, add improvisational material to expand upon the ideas, then polish each vignette a final time. After this rather tedious process, they listened to the taped dialogue in order to create the visuals they wanted for each segment.

During an interview, Dudley once detailed another phase of their script development; "We used to take headings down and then say, 'We need maybe to reverse this bit and that bit, put another bit in there, and then do it again.' And by process of elimination and addition, we'd come to the final order. More recently, I've gone straight to paper with my ideas—which I personally find more difficult—but sometimes it's useful

Cook and Moore relaxing on the set of "Bedazzled," 1967.

when one is blocked. It's good to have something facing you on a bit of paper. Although I feel that that's harder to change when you improvise into a tape recorder each time. But it's a mixture of the two things, really."

Not every skit made its way into the show, however. Cook remembers abandoning one segment which called for him to play a fairy cobbler, and Dudley as a Tinkerbell character. Unable to sufficiently flesh out the idea, they permanently shelved the sketch. Dudley also recalled another creation that never reached the London stage: "It was me made up as a black man singing 'Ol Man River' in a shower. The more I would sing,

the more my makeup would begin to wash off and the more my voice started to become English until, by the end, I was all white and started sounding like Noel Coward. Though the sketch did not appear in London, he and Cook snuck it in when *GOOD EVENING* played in America.

In Moore's opinion, the basis of their comedy as a team was to poke fun at the variable qualities of societal mores, life, and people. Unfortunately, not everyone was open-minded enough to appreciate (or, in some cases, to tolerate) much of the comedy found in *GOOD EVENING*. Without even touching on politics, the show managed to pro-

Lulu and Dudley Moore in BBC-TV's "It's Lulu, Not To Mention Dudley Moore," 1972.

voke a notable amount of public outrage, most of which came via the mail. Many angry letters were sent by religious groups, who were infuriated by the sacrilegious aspects of the "Gospel Truth" sketch. One man wrote that he loved *GOOD EVENING* until "the Holy Ghost came in, and then I felt I had to leave." Another theatregoer was more pointed in his letter, in which he declared that he was a devout Christian and asked Cook and Moore how they could make fun of the birth of Jesus Christ, adding, "May you burn in hell!"

The primary objection to Moore and Cook's broad comedic range was, in many other instances, the suspicion that these comic barbs were intended as a personal attack upon the parties or institutions they had chosen to satirize. Moore admitted that in comedy "there's always a slight attack implicit—but that the correct *attitude* makes a scene funny." None of the critics who reviewed the show found the birth of Christ spoof tasteless or offensive, and were noncommittal about its content, leaving it to the theatregoer to decide whether the piece was funny. Moore has said he would do the sketch again if the situation arose, since comedy, to paraphrase a line from one of Steve Martin's comedy albums, "isn't always pretty." In other words, comedy often has a deeper meaning, inspiring more than just laughter. It is the very quality, "a thinking man's comedy," that Cook and Moore enjoy inventing and performing for their audience.

Because *GOOD EVENING's* string of engagements became so exhausting, Dudley decided to return to his home in Islington after the show closed to take a badly needed rest. For once he wished for less work in order to concentrate more heavily on his piano compositions and other musical pursuits. Moore remarked in an interview at the time: "If I were feeling just a little active, I'd like to

play the piano in a small restaurant or club once a week with my trio, like I used to do. Swing, not avant-garde jazz, since that's so boring." Music figured strongly in his future and he hoped to soon write an opera for film adaptation.

Dudley's taste in music was changing, as was his taste in women. While touring with *GOOD EVENING* in 1973, Moore met the

Dudley attending the British premier of the film, "Lady Sings the Blues," 1973.

lovely, sexy actress Tuesday Weld and they began to date seriously. Tuesday and Dudley found that they had similarly unhappy childhoods in common. In fact, Tuesday claims never to have had a proper childhood at all since her show-business oriented mother involved her in child modeling from the age of three. Tuesday became her family's primary wage-earner (her father died during her infancy) and subsequently took advantage of the permissiveness which characterized her home life, eventually becoming known as Tuesday *Wild*, a reputation epitomized by her appearance on a nationally televised talk show barefoot, unkempt and clad in an old nightgown. Of her earlier years Tuesday has commented, ". . .I had the worst possible publicity. I decided to make up a whole life and say, 'Come on, follow me,' [to reporters] and I'd do the most outrageous things I could think of. Part of it was true, and I couldn't tell you which—it was done in total rebellion because they were intruding on my privacy. Not because I wasn't outrageous, because I

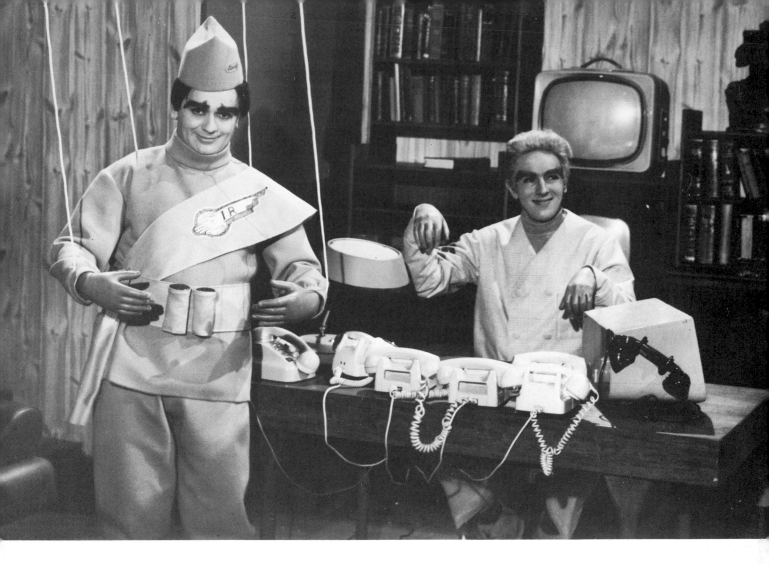

was. I'd just *vamp.* I'd do anything I could do to shock, and it became a part of me."

Tuesday, who was once described as a younger Marilyn Monroe, not surprisingly became one of the most talked about personalities in Hollywood. But the flurry of bad press over Tuesday's bohemian behavior had lessened considerably by the time she met Dudley. Newly divorced from Suzy Kendall, Dudley was free to pursue a relationship with Tuesday, which flourished, but not without some strife. As the romantic, albeit stormy, courtship became more serious, Tuesday announced that she was pregnant. While Dudley and Tuesday had not previously entertained the idea of marriage, her pregnancy provided the incentive they both had needed to take the step. In September of 1975, Dudley and Weld tied the marital knot in, of all places, Las Vegas, Nevada, the gam-

bling capital of the world. The couple then happily settled into Moore's spacious home in London.

In addition to the many aforementioned changes in Dudley's lifestyle, his long run in *GOOD EVENING* brought forth several new career challenges. In 1972, Dudley left the stage to star in two other productions: the first, an updated film version of *ALICE'S ADVENTURES IN WONDERLAND,* in which Moore plays the precocious Dormouse, and a BBC television special, *IT'S LULU—NOT TO MENTION, DUDLEY MOORE,* a comeback appearance for the singer Lulu.

ALICE'S ADVENTURES IN WONDERLAND was British film-maker William Sterling's rendition of the popular children's tale starring Fiona Fullerton in the title role as Alice and Michael Crawford as the White

left, **Peter Sellers as the March Hare, and Dudley Moore as the Doormouse, in "Alice's Adventures in Wonderland," 1972.**

Rabbit. Two former *GOON SHOW* members were also among the star-studded British cast—Peter Sellers as March Hare and Spike Milligan as Gryphon.

Unfortunately, this adaptation (Sterling directed and wrote the new screenplay) of the Lewis Carroll classic was a major box-office disappointment in which the talent of character actors and interesting special effects were largely wasted. Neither Moore's delightful performance nor the John Barry-Don Black score were able to save the production. The film, which opened in Los Angeles at Grauman's Chinese Theatre on November 8, 1972, took in a meager $35,000 on children's tickets during its first week, and, since such a poor showing did not bode well for the film, it swiftly disappeared from the country's movie circuit.

Nevertheless, 1972 had become the year during which Moore's career began to take hold, thanks to the laurels he had received for *GOOD EVENING*. Dudley was also working again with his first love, the piano, and soon formed the Dudley Moore Trio. His trio produced and recorded an album that same year for Atlantic Records called *TODAY*, which received credible reviews and established Dudley as a musical virtuoso. In 1973, Decca Records saw that Moore's career was picking up steam and decided to reissue one of his old vinyl recordings, *THE WORLD OF DUDLEY MOORE*. Then, in 1974, Dudley took advantage of the New York stage run of *GOOD EVENING*, to surprise everyone with an electrifying, impromptu performance at Michael's Pub in Manhattan (where Woody Allen often plays the clarinet in a Dixieland jazz band). Now Dudley began steering away from musical parodies to spend more time writing swing music. His reason? "Musical jokes are very difficult. Even Victor Borge has to talk more than play when he does his musical evenings." Dudley

went on to record ten jazz albums for American and British labels in the years to come.

Undeniably, Dudley was now in high gear and fine form. He and Peter Cook recorded an album based on their London stage show, *GOOD EVENING*, (Island Records), which was released in 1975. Even as their record shot up the sales charts, Moore and Cook were signed to record another comedy album, *DEREK AND CLIVE ALIVE*, which turned out to be their most controversial and the first to be banned in some record stores. Released in 1976, *DEREK AND CLIVE ALIVE* was partially live (from a performance at New York City's Bottom Line), with improvisational dialogue, and bore on the cover the following warning: "This record contains language of an explicit nature that may be offensive and should not be played in the presence of minors." Considering the comic reputation of Cook and Moore, fans must have thought the warning was some kind of inside joke, until, of course, they bought and listened to the album. What they heard was a compilation of sexually-oriented jokes, many of them exceedingly lewd, as well as outrageous one-liners and pointedly off-beat situations. Though the album was a perfect melange for those seeking this type of humor, to others, beware!

Dudley himself testifies that the Derek and Clive series (there were three albums: *DEREK AND CLIVE ALIVE*, *DEREK AND CLIVE CUMAGIN*, and *ADNAUSEUM*) was "the most obscene thing you've ever heard in your life...that's my mind. I'm a very *ribald* person. I enjoy a dirty joke, or a pun of scatalogical nature, 'cause it's all fun. I'm always baffled when puritanical shock comes over people's faces."

Moore and Cook once neglected their own record's warning, however, when they appeared at a function for a group of British

Tuesday Weld from an early film appearance in "The Gambler."

politicos. As Dudley later told *COSMO-POLITAN* about their lack of judgment: "Peter and I really failed. We did a thing for the Conservative Party in England for which we were getting paid royally, left everything to chance, and started improvising. Peter went off on this *obscene* impromptu tangent, and the room got colder and colder. Peter is relentless. He goes on till he makes people laugh, and there was no *way* anyone was going to laugh, so he kept on. I was just listening to him, thinking, 'Holy God, he is never going to get himself out of this.' And he didn't. The room was absolutely stony-faced. It was hilarious in retrospect, but a disaster. An *unbelievable* disaster."

Despite the occasional charges of bad taste, the Derek and Clive personae were successful for Cook and Moore. In Britain alone, *DEREK AND CLIVE ALIVE* sold over 50,000 albums just a few weeks after its release, and received instant cult acclaim. Four thousand copies were immediately exported to New York for distribution in the United States, and the record ultimately became the duo's biggest selling single album. That same year, taking advantage of the popularity engendered by the record's brisk sales, Moore and Cook took their unique comedy routines to American television by hosting one segment of the irreverent NBC late-night comedy show, *SATURDAY NIGHT LIVE*.

British television producers were also seeking the team's services again, and soon, producer Roger Graef signed Moore to narrate a Monty Python TV special entitled *PLEASURE AT HER MAJESTY'S*, which reunited many top British comedians at Her Majesty's Theatre in London's West End. The hour-long special was taped over a three-night period in the spring of 1976, and telecast in March 1977, bringing together for the first time in over ten years the original *BEYOND THE FRINGE* foursome of Peter

Cook, Jonathan Miller, Alan Bennett, and, of course, Dudley. Among the two dozen other celebrated funnymen who took the stage for this gala event were Michael Palin, John Cleese, John Bird, Terry Gilliam, Barry Humphries, Eleanor Bron, Graham Chapman, John Fortune, Graeme Garden, Neil Innes, Jonathan Lynn, Bill Odie and Tim Brooke-Taylor.

Moore's sophisticated, wily style as host and narrator caught the attention of producers Gary Herman and Penelope Gleming, who were planning an ABC documentary special, *TO THE QUEEN! A SALUTE TO ELIZABETH II*. Dudley accepted their offer to be one of a number of featured guests (including Peter Cook, Helen Marsh, and Jackie Stewart) in saluting and celebrating the reign of Queen Elizabeth II. Moore and Cook provided the necessary comic relief with some hilarious skits that spoofed the lifestyle of the Royal family.

Dudley had undoubtedly become one of the most sought-after comedians in the business, and even American film producers, forgetting the poor box-office performances of some of Dudley's earlier undertakings, were anxiously attempting to lure him back into feature films with an avalanche of offers. Luckily for them, Moore was ready for a fresh assault on the medium in which he had previously found no success, theatrical feature films. In late 1977 Moore was approached and eventually signed to the role of a sexually exasperated swinger, starring with Chevy Chase and Goldie Hawn in what became the comedy smash, *FOUL PLAY*. This marked Dudley's first film appearance in six years and his first American-produced film. Times had certainly changed since he had first begun making films in the late 1960s. Film properties had racier humor and the roles seemed meatier. *FOUL PLAY* was a kind of dream

Tuesday and Dudley Moore, 1975.

come true for Dudley, and was the first time American moviegoers would be able to enjoy the extent of Dudley's talent in the role that seemed so suited to him.

Although Hollywood and New York are the usual locales for film premieres, FOUL PLAY upset that tradition by holding its world-wide debut at San Francisco's regal Palace of Fine Arts on July 9, 1978. This was only fitting, since FOUL PLAY had been filmed mostly in the Bay Area. It marked the first time in 12 years that the city had staged a gala Hollywood premiere. The result: an overflowing, standing room only crowd of over 1100 stars, dignitaries, studio executives, and a mob of fans outside cheering the arrivals of Chevy Chase, Burgess Meredith, Dudley, Billy Barty, and many others. Goldie Hawn was the only cast member who did not make an appearance since she was filming another project in Europe. Inside the theatre, the biggest round of applause went to Cyril Magnin, one of the city's most influential citizens, who appears in the film as the Pope. Monies from this lavish affair helped benefit the San Francisco Spring Opera Theatre and the American Conservatory Theatre.

While San Franciscans already knew the film would be successful, FOUL PLAY opened several days later in New York and Los Angeles to more sellout crowds. Critics were generous with their praise, applauding the comedy thriller's sense of fun. They especially enjoyed director-screenwriter Colin Higgins' borrowed car chase scene from BULLITT with Steve McQueen, and the reworked bits and pieces of Alfred Hitchcock thrillers VERTIGO and THE MAN WHO KNEW TOO MUCH. Higgins, whose previous hit was Gene Wilder's SILVER STREAK, also earned pats on the back for his precise direction and lively use of supporting characters like Billy Barty as a Bible-toting sales-man, Burgess Meredith as Hawn's kindly landlord, William Frankfeather as the villainous Albino, and Marc Lawrence and Don Calfa as the henchmen.

As for Dudley, well...Dudley stole the show. As NEWSWEEK'S David Ansen wrote: "The comic laurels, however, go to the pint-sized Dudley Moore as a closet swinger eternally caught in kinkiness interruptus by endangered Goldie; it's a crude running gag, which Moore milks for more than it's worth." With so much happening in FOUL PLAY, the film became a major box-office power, grossing more than $70 million.

In FOUL PLAY, a divorced San Francisco librarian, Gloria Mundy (Goldie Hawn), is being chased by a nefarious underworld criminal, the Dwarf, whose interest in her is retrieving an incriminating roll of film, that she does not know is in her possession. Tony Carlson (Chevy Chase), a wise-cracking, affable local police lieutenant, is assigned to protect Mundy from the Dwarf and his henchmen, and here the escapades begin.

Moore emerges as the chubby, sex-starved maniac, Stanley Tibbets, when he meets Gloria in Twosomes, a local singles bar. Gloria, slipping into the club to elude one of the Dwarf's henchmen, and unaware of the club's unsavory reputation, explains to Tibbets that she needs to find a safe hideout nearby. Tibbets, possibly the most under-sexed man in San Francisco, interprets her explanation as an open-invitation for him to spend the night with her, and willingly takes her into his apartment. He is not about to turn down such an eager offer from someone as irresistible as Goldie Hawn!

Back at his bachelor's pad, Moore turns on his charm, offering Mundy a drink, turning on his at-home discotheque, and making his ultimate intentions very clear indeed. As he dances gleefully to the insistent pounding of a disco tune, he then unveils his array

Dudley Moore as Stanley Tibbets, conductor, in "Foul Play," 1978.

of pleasure-props; plastic blow-up women, foldout beds, and golden statuettes. Tibbets then makes advances on Gloria (she's oblivious to Dudley's mounting passion, and peeks continually out of the window watching for Albino), stripping down to his colorful boxer shorts. When Gloria finally realizes what Dudley has in mind she is aghast. Stanley apologizes with only moderate sincerity; after all, his "sure thing" has become another letdown.

Tibbets' romantic failures turn into the film's running gag. Towards the middle of the film, Gloria, still running from the Dwarf's cronies, ducks into a house of ill repute only to find Stanley engrossed in blue movies. She informs a startled Stanley of her predicament and asks for his help. Though Tibbets is extremely hesitant at first when he considers the result of his last efforts, he suddenly becomes brazen enough to call for the police to stage a raid in the hopes that the Dwarf's men will be arrested. When Moore sneaks out to phone the police, he accidentally bumps into the two bruisers, who proceed to dump the unfortunate character into a whirlpool bath just for standing in their way. Gloria engineers her own escape, while Stanley remains at the mercy of the goons. When the police finally make their appearance, they promptly arrest Moore and the other paying customers for indecent exposure.

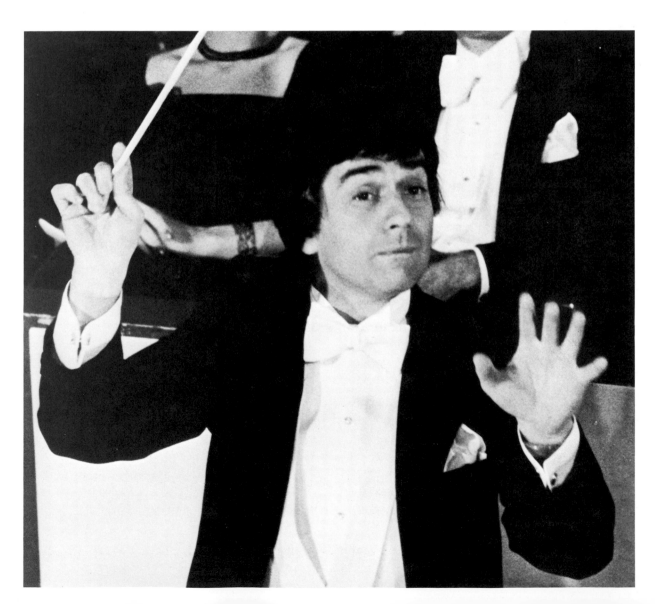

A fitting conclusion to this madcap comedy comes with the end of the film, as the Roman Catholic pontiff, Pope John II, attends a special performance of a major musical symphony downtown. The conductor for the symphony is none other than Stanley Tibbets. Bedlam spreads quickly as Lt. Carlson (who by this time has a *romantic* interest in rescuing Gloria from the clutches of her captor, Albino), arrives in time to foil Albino's plot to assassinate the Pope.

Following this triumph, Carlson and Gloria are reunited backstage, and they embrace, when suddenly the curtain is raised and the audience beholds their kiss. When the befuddled Tibbets spots Gloria for a *third* time, he quickly dons a pair of sunglasses so he may finish conducting the symphony incognito rather than risk another encounter with unlucky Gloria.

FOUL PLAY received a stream of good notices, with Dudley's performance repeatedly gaining special attention. Combined with his earlier stage and recording triumphs, Moore was finally making his mark in Hollywood and in the show business world, providing him with ample compensation for his years of struggle. For once, Dudley was at

Peter Cook and Dudley Moore as Sherlock Holmes and Dr. Watson in "The Hound of the Baskervilles," 1978.

peace with himself and enjoying his new-found success.

Moore did, however, make one mistake along the way. A project he had filmed a year earlier, and had all but forgotten about was a British movie spoof of *THE HOUND OF THE BASKERVILLES*, and starred Dudley and Peter Cook as the legendary detective team, Sherlock Holmes and Dr. Watson. This twelfth remake of the Sir Arthur Conan Doyle tale, was co-written by Cook and director Paul Morrissey, who also scored the music.

Dudley contends that the picture was "a tough collaboration," and blames the film's failure on the unorthodox Morrissey (also responsible for the gruesome Andy Warhol remake of *FRANKENSTEIN*), with whom he disagreed on the subject of comedy. *THE HOUND OF THE BASKERVILLES*, which might have been a perfect comedy vehicle for Cook and Moore, ultimately became their worst offering to the world of comic cinema.

The film calls for Peter Cook to essay a comic rendition of Sherlock Holmes; hairnet and dressing gown completed his attire. Meanwhile, Dudley was cast in multiple roles, first as Cook's moronic assistant, Dr. Watson, then as Mr. Spiggot, a hopping one-legged lunatic (yet another resurrection of the *BEYOND THE FRINGE* character), and finally as Sherlock's Mum, Sheryl (imagine a buxom Dudley!).

This satire seemed funny on paper, but failed to transfer its sparkle to celluloid. The film contained no real plot, but was instead separated into different crime-solving episodes, the only link being the Holmes-Watson characters, and the film fell flat immediately. The humor was an uninspired meld of bad puns, double entendres, and lavatory humor. For instance, one sequence depicted Holmes attempting to squeeze information from one of his informers that would lead to the identity of the person who took a part of St. Beryl, a local museum mummy. The relic in question was a mummified elbow. As Sherlock deduces rather quickly, "It was almost certainly the work of thieves."

One sketch deserves at least a passing mention. In an outlandish "Exorcist" takeoff, co-star Joan Greenwood bares her bosom, which flashes "Love Me" in neon, turns one eye reflecting red, the other green, and produces a tongue similar to those unraveling party favors, all as part of the exorcism ritual. The scene then goes beyond any limitations the serious American version may have had by staging an excessively repulsive pea soup vomit fight!

Critics "hounded" Cook, Moore and Morrissey for subjecting filmgoers to such easily forgettable satire. As a critic for *DAILY VARIETY* declared: "Cook and Moore have deteriorated into almost complete reliance on lavatory humor to get laughs." David Chute of the *LOS ANGELES HERALD-EXAMINER* added: "The Movie is crass and clumsy and its jokes fizzle more often than snap."

Dudley was fortunate that the film tarnished his career only slightly in the United Kingdom, where the film was released in 1978, and hardly at all in the U.S., where American audiences were spared many screening due to a minor distribution in Hollywood only. *FOUL PLAY* was still Dudley's claim to stateside success. Indeed, he had almost become a household name, as women found him sexy and attractive and wished he would accept another film part soon. Hollywood producers began offering him lead roles for feature films, instead of the cameo, or even co-starring roles he had been used to in the past. With his services now being sought so fervently, Dudley carefully planned his next conquest; a movie that would ultimately rate him a '10' among all male actors.

CHAPTER 5

"The Making of a '10'"

Dudley's rise to full-fledged stardom was long overdue. He had certainly paid his dues to the film world, with performances ranging from splendid to sordid. It was time for Dudley to break away from the up and down, see-saw pattern that had characterized his career thus far. By now, Moore wanted to *stay* on top.

Just why his career was so mercurial had always escaped Dudley, though recently he admitted that perhaps the right breaks did not come early enough in his career to establish him in the eyes of the public as a high-bracket star. Instead, he was forced to take so many chances that he was inevitably involved in a few failures. Moore also believes that he might not have been able to handle large-scale success earlier in his life. Since he was always trying to understand his idiosyncrasies, he was perhaps unable to withstand the pressure, and these emotional uncertainties, combined with an irrepressibly high ambition, kept his career constantly on the edge until FOUL PLAY. The year 1978 will undoubtedly go down in show business annals as the second most productive year of Moore's career, matching his previous high in 1971 when GOOD EVENING initiated his short-lived revival. Following his sensational performance in FOUL PLAY Dudley landed starring roles in a string of film and television productions that had very little effect on his career, but kept him visible while he waited for a role to equal his success as Stanley Tibbets.

Moore guest-starred on an ABC television special, *US AGAINST THE WORLD II*, which featured a dazzling roster of film and television superstars in a sports competition. Filmed in Valencia, California at the Magic Mountain amusement park, and telecast on September 9, 1978, the special pitted a team of United States athletes against a "world" team comprised of superstars William Shatner, Bo Svenson, Rich Little, LeVar Burton, Britt Ekland, Victoria Principal, Jane Seymour, Fionnuala Flanagan, Oleg Cassini, Sivi Aberg, Paul Nicholas, and the one and only Dudley Moore. Hosting the events were Ed McMahon (of *THE TONIGHT SHOW* with Johnny Carson), Ted Knight, and Gabriel Kaplan. Dudley's participation in these games harked back to his childhood days of rough rugby matches, but Dudley must have found teammates Britt and Victoria more pleasing on the pitch than the powerhouse preppies of his Oxford days. And although this special was not intended to be a major boon to his career, Moore was not one to frown on such offers. The show clearly served one purpose alone; to widen his scope of appeal with television viewers who had only seen his jocular performance in *FOUL PLAY* or knew absolutely nothing at all about him. His prayers that the program would do both were instantly answered as a stream of offers poured in from producers. Television and newspaper reporters also noticed and interviewed Dudley and began writing a plethora of feature articles about his struggle to succeed after years of hardship and unhappiness.

An understandably jolly Dudley Moore and Bo Derek in a scene from "10," 1979.

Still faithful to his music, Dudley released a new album, *THE DUDLEY MOORE TRIO*, a recording of his 1978 performance at the Sydney, Australia Town Hall, which has become a popular seller in many parts of the world. Moore's jazz LP features a remarkable range of selections, including the old standards *"Here's That Rainy Day,"* and *"Autumn in New York,"* plus several original compositions. Of the disc, Dudley comments: "I play entirely from the heart and I love it only when I do play. My music is self-taught at this point. I have a facile technique that I work to perfect. I particularly love improvising, but what I adore most is accompanying singers, people like Dakota Staton, Mel Torme, and Jimmy Rushing. I love to play for singers. A dream of mine has been to play for Peggy Lee."

Though pleased with his music, and still fresh from *FOUL PLAY*, a strange sense of emptiness seemed to plague Moore at this juncture. Despite the celebration of his fourth year with Tuesday Weld and his son, Patrick, the marriage was showing signs of wear. Tuesday and Dudley often exploded into childish arguments, sometimes over petty things, but, according to Moore, "She kept me honest." These usually small-scale feuds sometimes became quite serious, however, and were the cause of the couple's eventual separation.

Moore has commented that his main conflict at this time was with himself, specifically, his outlook on life and his identity. He was still under the impression that he did not understand himself, and wasn't sure what he wanted out of life. Significant dilemmas indeed, but nothing new to Dudley—in fact, his entire life has been plagued with the combination of accomplishment and insecurity.

Dudley was entering the third phase of his life and career, which had experienced a rejuvenation thanks to the success of *FOUL PLAY*. The first portion of Dudley's professional life had centered around one main task: publicity and being noticed. In the 1960s with *BEYOND THE FRINGE* and along with Peter Cook on their weekly BBC series, Dudley found his way into the limelight. The results were satisfying, but not overwhelming enough to insure a steady flow of offers from agents and producers. Meanwhile, his marriage to Suzy Kendall had collapsed, creating additional problems. Moore's second phase was just as much of a challenge. While his second marriage to Tuesday Weld crumbled, his career enjoyed a new high with the successes of *GOOD EVENING* and *FOUL PLAY*, only to suffer a setback when his involvement with *THE HOUND OF THE BASKERVILLES* came to the attention of the critics and barred any further advances. This new period of Dudley's life helped to ease his tensions, but did not solve all of the problems that so frequently tormented him.

Throughout most of his career, Dudley attended weekly group therapy sessions and had been undergoing psychoanalysis for some time. (In fact, his therapy had begun during adolescence because as a child he would compare his abilities to those of other kids, and ended up feeling inadequate.) In Beverly Hills he attended therapy sessions where he met new people, some of whom were Hollywood producers and celebrities like himself, who faced problems at home or were battling with their own identities. Dudley had become interested in psychoanalytic techniques during his adolescence, and his fervor for discovering the source of his frustrations never lessened. He traced many of his fears back to his childhood, of which he has remarked, "My parents didn't understand the dangers of leaving me that alone...I got a real fear of abandonment, which is basically my worst fear, but from

A happy family: Dudley Moore, baby Patrick and Tuesday Weld in 1977.

what I learned in group therapy, it seems to be mostly everybody's." It was during these sessions that Dudley became good friends with Blake Edwards, known for his production of the PINK PANTHER films with the incomparable Peter Sellers.

Edwards was in the midst of casting his latest picture, THE FERRET, an Inspector Clouseau spin-off that he had planned to develop into a new series like THE PINK PANTHER, featuring Peter Sellers in the title role. But Sellers suffered a fatal heart attack, which postponed the film project until Edwards met Moore. One afternoon Edwards made a suggestion to Dudley during their talks, "I sat there watching him for some time and thought, 'He'd be just marvelous as 'THE FERRET,'" Edwards recalled. "And when I discussed it with Dudley he was equally enthusiastic. The great thing about him is that he's a talented writer as well as a good actor. So if the film took off—and one is always hoping for sequels—then he'd prove invaluable."

But Dudley and Edwards had had an "encounter" well before their days of group therapy. Edwards, when reminded of the posh Hollywood party where they first met, recalled, "Yes, Dudley and I were at the same party and he was demonstrating how various nationalities throw up. When we met again in group therapy, the vibes were just so good. Meeting Dudley was the best thing to happen to me since Pete Ustinov walked out on the original PINK PANTHER film."

Dudley was apparently delighted over Edwards' interest in him and agreed to try the role of the famous underground agent, under the condition that he would not be forced to do any sequels. Since Moore did not want to become typecast, he persuaded Edwards that a series of films would not be as successful.

In THE FERRET, Dudley was to play the son of a famous World War II agent whose code name is the Ferret. Well-fed and bred in Britain by his mother, Moore is sent back to the warfront to help his father, who is in trouble. Although he does not know what to do with guns, and fears that kind of action, Dudley assumes the moniker of the Ferret when his father is killed, thus creating the premise for the sequence of hilarious events that follow. As Edwards later admitted, "Obviously, comparisons with the Panther will be inevitable. But, in fact, the principal character will be nothing at all like Clouseau. Much more in the Harold Lloyd tradition: not so much a fumbler as inept. I want this to be more a suspense comedy than the sort of burlesque, slapstick, stuff I did with the PANTHERS."

With Dudley scheduled to star in THE FERRET, Edwards had to make a last minute change in another film when actor George Segal stormed off the set of Edwards' new comedy, 10, which featured one of Hollywood's brightest, most beautiful newcomers, Bo Derek. According to Edwards, Segal walked off the Metro Goldwyn Mayer studio lot the first day of filming in a dispute over the amount of control his wife was to have as associate producer of the production. Edwards and Segal were extremely volatile personalities, and they clashed instantly when the subject arose during a conversation. Segal, in an eleventh-hour decision, left the production the next day. Orion Pictures, the production company in charge, objected to Segal's unexpected and unauthorized departure by filing a legal action suit against the actor seeking damages totaling over $11.5 million. Segal furiously countersued for $10 million.

With the entire case awaiting court review, Edwards made a surprise maneuver by pulling Moore from THE FERRET and casting him instead in the title role of 10. (Because of Segal's legal maneuver Edwards

was eventually forced to cancel production of *THE FERRET* due to script and budget restraints.) In *10*, Dudley would play George Webber, a forty-two-year-old man suffering from a mid-life crisis who feels that a younger, "ideal," woman is the only solution to his problem. The sequence of episodes leading up to the meeting between Dudley and Bo Derek are now classic bits of comedy. Moore was given the chance to be Chaplin, Keaton and himself all at the same time.

Edwards' first draft of the screenplay for *10* featured Segal as a Beverly Hills dentist troubled with "male menopause." But the dentist character was quickly transformed into that of an award-winning songwriter,

which suited Dudley perfectly. When the script changes were finalized, Edwards began the 16 week filming schedule on November 6, 1978, which took the cast to Los Angeles and Mexico.

During a break in the filming, Moore pointed out that the task of playing George Webber was a difficult one. He credits the character's believability to Blake Edwards, for allowing a more natural evolution of character development, rather than imposing a preconceived idea of how the Webber persona should be played. Says Dudley: "I think when '10' came along, it was a conjunction of my personal and professional life. I came up with who I was and went with it. I felt com-

Derek, Moore and Julie Andrews out for a stroll in "10," 1979.

fortable in the role just playing myself. So I decided to allow that part of myself in my work and any other vulnerabilities that might suddenly arise. I remember talking to Blake about it because I wasn't sure how I wanted to play the character, but I felt it would be better if I played it straight. He agreed and I felt fine doing it because I didn't have to put on a voice or a funny walk, which I had always done in my other work."

Webber's character mirrored Dudley's, as they were both going through almost identical mid-life experiences. "The dilemma that George Webber finds himself in in *10* is something that I've struggled with, in one way or another, forever. Not only in terms of personal relationships but in dealing with life in general—coming to reality of things and people," Moore confessed. This was why Moore did not have to prepare very much for the role. Instead, he waited until filming actually began before he started thinking in terms of what he would do in a particular scene. Spontaneity best describes the magical, harmonious blend between the carefree style with which Blake Edwards directed the film and Dudley's improvisational abilities. As Dudley tells it: "He doesn't direct, which is great. I hate being directed. He just sort of lets you do it. We didn't really discuss scenes very much, except for the bedroom scene with Bo Derek, when we're seen talking in bed."

That particular episode required Moore to strip down to his birthday suit for the second time in the film. (His first nude entrance occurred during a sex party.) Edwards had originally agreed that Dudley would fake his participation in the sequence by wrapping a towel around his genitals. But Edwards finally decided that Dudley should do the scene in the buff. In order to cement his courage, Dudley closed his eyes, but couldn't think of anything except what his mother would say about the semi-pornographic scene that the public would see. As he proudly recalled later, "My first nude scene. A moment of high drama, naturally. Normally there are about six guys behind the camera, but when I peeled off there must have been fifty of them, all waiting for me to give my all. The lighting cameraman went into hysterics. I'd have felt pretty silly standing there with a towel 'round me. So I took everything off. When I got home that night, I had a delayed reaction. I suddenly sat up in bed horrified. Had I really done that?"

Dudley was also known as a compulsive eater between films and needed to diet before filming *10* in order to trim off some unsightly pounds. At one time he was quite slender, but, as he quipped, "I can't remember how I got that way; must have had something removed." Since Dudley also had a weakness for gourmet cooking, and considers eating a fine dinner "one of the great pleasures of life," his dieting was, in his words, "the battle of the bulge." His motivation to lose weight, he says, came from within: "I suffer when I look at myself on the screen with bulges, so I get very disciplined about reducing well before doing a picture." His strict low-calorie diet was comprised of either fish or chicken, three vegetables, cottage cheese, a choice of fruit, low-cal jam, and pistachio nuts. The results of Moore's program: he lost 18 pounds in 18 days and felt better as a person. "I felt so well fed that when I started my day I didn't think of food again. But sometimes I went to bed early and dreamed of my morning feast." In the ensuing years, Dudley has been known to rely upon a two-trout breakfast, his only meal of the day, to knock off the creeping poundage, but is happiest with his favorite fare of Mai Tais and frankfurters.

Dudley's trim, new physique enabled him to put every bit of his energy into his performance as George Webber, and for good reason; Dudley was receiving a weighty salary, more than $1 million (or about 600,000 English pounds).

Moore's hard-earned fitness allowed him to perform many risky stunts without the aid of a double. He did enough physically exhausting scenes to make any stuntman proud, such as saving a man twice his size from a shark, tumbling backwards over the side of a cliff, toppling into a swimming pool, and struggling helplessly up a steep hill, all for the sake of romance.

These antics and the mystique of the Bo Derek character made 10 the talk of show business. Film critics were tabbing the 1979 Christmas film season as the year of "escapist movie entertainment," which perhaps helped Americans forget the senseless ordeal of the United States Embassy hostages in Iran. Some of the blockbuster films released that season were Steve Martin's *THE JERK*, Peter Sellers' *BEING THERE*, the Dustin Hoffman/Meryl Streep tearjerker *KRAMER VS. KRAMER*, and the Robert Redford/Jane Fonda adventure, *THE ELECTRIC HORSEMAN*. Probably the biggest sensation of all was 10.

The film's box-office fireworks were almost beyond comprehension. 10 earned more than $60 million worldwide and went on to become an industry of its own! Bo Derek's "cornrow" hairstyle became a standard commodity at hair salons the world over. Bo's husband/Svengali, John Derek, capitalized on his wife's phenomenal appeal by merchandising a million-selling poster of his young movie queen, titillating the sexual taste buds of men of all ages. And Dudley, lauded by critics as the primary reason for 10's success, earned the flattering title of filmdom's "newest and sexiest male star," following in the tradition of Cary Grant and Marcello Mastroianni. To his devout female fans, Moore could do no wrong, offering them what super-macho stars like Burt

Reynolds or Clint Eastwood didn't, a sensitive, compassionate, humble quality that was real, not fantasy.

10 begins with a surprise party for its guest of honor, George Webber, an award-winning, smart-aleck songwriter celebrating his forty-second birthday. The party is organized by "Sam," Samantha Taylor (Julie Andrews), a thirty-eight-year-old feminist singer who has established a poignant, firm relationship with George. Although he's considered the most successful Hollywood songsmith around, his collaborator Hugh (Robert Webber), a homosexual, disrupts Dudley's good mood by remarking that he's noticed some peculiar changes in George's behavior. Apparently, George has become obsessed with old age, going through what Hugh calls "male menopause" or mid-life crisis. Needless to say, George becomes somewhat morose. Webber would like to halt the progression of his age, and wants instead to return to his youthful days of seducing young women and never having to worry about his future. George decides that he must find some answers, and possibly a few adventures, to cure himself of this dilemma.

During an afternoon drive, he stops alongside a limousine carrying a gorgeous woman, gowned and heading towards her wedding. George becomes instantly entranced, feeling that he's discovered the antidote to what ails him; the perfect woman of the world, an 11 on a scale of 10. (She's so good, he feels, that she rates higher than the scale will permit.) His heart quivering, George sets off in hot, hilarious pursuit of the woman, Jenny (Bo Derek). His frantic chase turns hazardous as he accidentally drives his Rolls Royce down a one way street, crashing into a parked police car. While Jenny calmly glides into the church where she's to be married, George is left to deal with the police, who charge him with reckless driving and

driving an unregistered auto without a valid license. George clearly has more than just sexual problems.

George resumes following Jenny, sneaking into the church to peer at the proceedings from behind an expensive flower arrangement near the altar. Mesmerized by Jenny's overwhelming beauty, George does not notice the inquisitive bee which springs from the flowers to sting his nose. The pain causes him to stumble over the exquisite flower bouquet, catching the eye of every churchgoer, including Jenny and her husband-to-be, David Henley (Sam Jones). Hugely embarrassed, George dashes out of the church to safety.

That evening, after dinner with Samantha, George is still haunted by the vision of the heavenly Jenny. He steps outside to his patio, where a telescope offers a view of an orgy next door. Continual spying on his neighbor's sexploits only compounds George's crisis, however. Why isn't he having any fun? Later, Samantha and George tangle in a bedroom argument over the definition of "broad," which he insists isn't slang for "woman." Sam, infuriated at his chauvinism and ignorance, storms off, leaving a confused Webber to sleep alone.

With Sam temporarily gone, George seizes the opportunity to quest after Jenny Henley. The task is not so easy—remember, the newlyweds are on their honeymoon, and could be anywhere from Paris to Tahiti! Dudley's comic chase takes him first to the zealous reverend who conducted the marriage ceremonies. The minister, though, turns out to be one of George's biggest fans and tries impressing him with some piano playing. Dudley deadpans through the pastor's atrocious mini-recital. Only when the "performance" is over does the minister awaken to why George is visiting him, he wants to find Jenny.

Bo Derek, whose assets need no description, and Dudley from "10," 1979.

Apparently, Jenny's father is one of the most prominent dentists in all of Beverly Hills and, according to the reverend, would know Jenny's approximate whereabouts. George promptly schedules an appointment to have his teeth checked, in order to discover where the dentist's lovely daughter might be. Instead, he is informed that he has six cavities, all of which the dentist fills during the visit. George emerges drugged from Novocaine shots and with cheeks so puffy that he resembles a chipmunk. Adding to the pain is the knowledge that Jenny is in the far off tropical retreat of Acapulco. His dedication (and teeth) still intact, George decides that no distance is too far to roam for the chance to make love to Jenny, and he boards a plane for Mexico.

Miraculously, and to his utter delight, George soon finds Jenny sunbathing on a beach. He tries to avoid a scene as he approaches her, but this is a *comedy* film, and Dudley has only begun to roll. As he runs towards Jenny, the excruciating heat of the sand causes him to jump up and down like a Mexican jumping bean, surely a conspicuous sight. With the aid of two towels placed under his feet for protection, George comically lurches towards Jenny, moving the towels under his tootsies as he advances.

George does not always play the buffoon, however. His heroics are really what persuade the buxom Jenny to notice him for the first time, as George saves Jenny's husband from drowning! With David hospitalized, Jenny wastes little time in getting to know George, first dining with him, then seducing him to the classical tune of Ravel's *Bolero* (it's the only song Jenny makes love to). During these intensely romantic scenes, director Blake Edwards tastefully blends eroticism with comedy. Some hysterical scenarios arise when Jenny and George begin to make love; the Bolero record skips (caus-

ing a stark naked George to hop out of bed to restart it), the telephone rings (it's David calling to check up on Jenny), and George and Jenny have difficulty finding comfortable sexual positions. Finally, (and this becomes the movie's main message), George realizes that although Jenny rates a 10 physically, her bland personality lessens her value considerably. His fantasy shattered, Dudley wonders if a real 10 exists anywhere. Of course she does, as he finds with Samantha when they have a lovemaking patch-up upon his return home.

In *10*, Dudley displayed a human, sophisticated side that had been missing in previous films. George Webber had turned out to be a character almost identical to his own, appearing exquisitely suave, humble, mischievous, and often childlike. And Dudley's musical prowess was again realized during the segments in which he played his beloved piano. The kudos heaped upon him were richly deserved. It would be an understatement to say that *10* was a timely career shift for Dudley. Much more than that, he had finally "arrived."

In addition, co-star Julie Andrews had broken out of her goody goody image to give a strong performance as Samantha. And of course, Bo Derek as the model, ideal woman became a worldwide sensation and one of the hottest female properties to come out of Hollywood in a long time. As Dudley remarked about the Derek-delirium: "I'm delighted what's happened to Bo. A lot has been written about her, some of it critical. I don't agree. She's very sweet, charming, and seems very uncomplicated. I suspect she's also a natural actress—you'd have to be to do so well at twenty-three." Finally, director Blake Edwards received applause for carefully supervising a tender subject matter in a way that did more to entertain than offend. His

CHAPTER 6

"It's Awful To Be Alone"
—Arthur

Dudley fell in love with the next script he was offered— a biblical spoof originally called *THE BOOK OF HERSCHEL* but later renamed *WHOLLY MOSES!* Moore was cast in the lead role as a befuddled Egyptian idolmaker, Herschel, whose struggle against destiny (and a rival by the name of Moses), to try and become the leader of the Chosen People creates the meat of the plot. "It's a part in which I can be me," said Dudley. "And that is what I've been working for all these years—to be myself." Dudley was no stranger to religious farce, since his *GOOD EVENING* stage show had included the satirization of the birth of Jesus. The concerns of *WHOLLY MOSES!* were much broader; its good-natured irreverence was aimed at everything in sight!

The film's director, new to feature film direction, was Gary Weis, who has previously piloted segments for NBC's popular *SATURDAY NIGHT LIVE*. Guy Thomas penned the original screenplay, which Charles H. Joffe produced for Columbia Pictures. Filming began on October 22, 1979, in the Lancaster-Palmdale high desert regions of California, with Dudley and a rather prominent cast of film and television personalities including James Coco, Paul Sand, Madeline Kahn, John Ritter, and Dom Deluise.

The euphoria of stardom and a new film project was tainted, however, by discontented rumblings at the Moore household. Dudley's marriage to Tuesday Weld could no longer be saved, and after five years together they mutually decided to call it quits. The couple reportedly fought, off and on for many years, with periodic separations to help smooth problems over when necessary.

In April of 1980, Tuesday made their last separation final when she filed for divorce. Moore's main concern was for his four-year-old son, Patrick, and how the divorce would affect him. The settlement revolved around what was best for Patrick, and, as Dudley once remarked, "I was very afraid of the idea of a child. Then it happened, and I must say, it's the best thing that's ever happened to me. Once it happened, I loved it. If I had my way, though, I probably wouldn't have had him. But Tuesday wanted to—and there he was."

Tuesday's legal proceedings against him came as no surprise, however, as Moore explained, "We were too tempestuous, although tempestuous is too romantic a word to describe our relationship. But we did know how to fight nicely. Marriage is an arena where you fight as adults all your problems as children. We were always arguing and fighting. It made life interesting and sort of exhausting."

Moore admitted that his separation from Tuesday was better for him, personally, since he functions more efficiently when alone. His own problem, he says, is "my contribution to the mismanagement of my relationships. Anyone hidden like me is difficult to live with." Dudley likewise confesses that Tuesday and he were never easy on each other. "In many ways, I think we challenged each other all the time. In a sense, she's very

75

perceptive about feelings and if she felt I was trying to disguise something, she would challenge me by being humorous or by teasing me or whatever. But now I realize that's not a bad thing, necessarily. We were fighting for a purpose. There was nothing wrong with it."

While the divorce proceedings dragged on, Moore was surely hopeful that *WHOLLY MOSES!* would live up to his fans' and his own expectations. With *10* still a box-office smash, Dudley was convinced that his upcoming picture had to measure up to *10*'s performance. And *WHOLLY MOSES!* seemed to contain sure-fire ingredients to insure back-to-back triumphs for him: a strong leading role backed by a popular cast, and a plot that seemed to have universal appeal. The result? A critical turkey, but a box office surprise.

WHOLLY MOSES! made its screen debut at four Hollywood cinemas on June 13, 1980 to an avalanche of bad reviews. The film amazed critics and film executives, however, with its gross dollar count at theaters following its nationwide opening. At first it was thought that the curiosity generated by another successful biblical "epic," Monty Python's *LIFE OF BRIAN*, sent film fans to see *WHOLLY MOSES!* Whatever the case, the film tallied very impressive figures during its first three days, even surpassing over a period of time two of the summer season's most touted releases, John Travolta's *URBAN COWBOY* and Clint Eastwood's *BRONCO BILLY.*

Columbia Pictures, the distributor of *WHOLLY MOSES!*, reported that the film amassed a healthy $3,681,649 at 611 theaters in three days in the United States and Canada. Of that amount, $445,028 was yielded from 62 New York cinemas and $211,789 from 45 Hollywood locations. When broken down even further, *WHOLLY MOSES!* was averaging almost $6,000 per theater nationally, which was not at all bad for a critical catastrophe. During comparable lengths of time, *WHOLLY MOSES!* notched $23,368 in three days at Hollywood's Paramount Theatre while *BRONCO BILLY* rolled up $9,560 at the Fox Theatre and *URBAN COWBOY* drew $17,329 at Grauman's Chinese Theatre. There seemed to be only one possible explanation for the film's initial box office madness, and that was the phenomenal drawing power of its star, Dudley Moore.

But even Dudley was not enough to keep the movie's box-office supremacy for long. When a comedy film's funniest sequences are at the beginning and at the end, it is bound to have a short life in the theatres. *WHOLLY MOSES!* is just such a movie.

The film begins in Egypt with Harvey (Dudley), a New York college language studies professor, bound for the Holy Land on a no-frills tourist bus. (Harvey was originally headed for Paris, but his travel agent had fouled up his plans.) Moore sets the comedy wheels in motion by being the last to board the bus, getting his head caught in the door. As the dilapidated Greyhound-reject roars off, poor Dudley is flailing his arms and screaming for the driver to stop. Unfortunately, this slapstick gag is about as funny as the movie gets.

After this dubious opening, Dudley and his traveling companion Zoey (Laraine Newman), get sidetracked during a desert stopover into a cavern where they discover the "Book of Herschel." This ancient scroll recounts the life of the son of a slave who falls under the impression that it is he (and *not* Moses) who is the Chosen One to lead God's people out of bondage.

With Moore narrating, the film flashes back to Pharaonic times, wherein a decree has just been served stating that every child

amongst the Chosen shall be slain. In order to protect the innocent lives of these children, the parents cast them afloat in man-made arks down the Nile River in the hopes that their children will reach safety, preferably the home of the Pharaoh (played by Richard Pryor), whose wife longs for a child of her own. Among the concerned parents is Hyssop (James Coco), whose son Herschel's raft takes a wrong turn, accidentally landing in the hands of the Senment family (idolmakers who operate a shop under the slogan, "Idol Makers Since the Flood"). When Hyssop hears of his son's whereabouts, he becomes one of the Senment's slaves so he can stay close to Herschel.

Herschel (Dudley in a dual role) grows up and eventually cuts all ties with his father

and the idolmaking business and goes off on his own. His journey takes him to the land of a shepherd, Jethro of Mee, where he joins the family and marries one of Jethro's daughters, Zerelda (Laraine Newman in a dual role), whom Herschel had met previously while working at his idolmaker's shop.

As sheepherding begins to lose its sparkle, Herschel turns his attention to serving God and his dream of being the Chosen People's leader. One afternoon, Moses, a member of the same family, is lost with his flock, and Jethro orders Herschel to find the boy. The search leads Herschel high up a mountainside where he smells, but cannot see, a burning bush, none other than the proverbial bush where God is speaking to a kneeling Moses, appointing *him* to free the

Laraine Newman, Dudley Moore and Jack Gilford from "Wholly Moses!"

Chosen People. Herschel comes upon the scene just as God has begun to give his instructions, and with Moses hidden from view, Herschel thinks God is speaking to *him.*

The remaining storyline focuses on Herschel's attempts to accomplish the holy task. Only he is one savior too late, since Moses has already done the job. A short time after this anti-climax the film comes out of flashback to show Harvey and Zoey reboarding the bus, with Dudley again catching his head in the door.

None of the gags from *WHOLLY MOSES!* will ever make the Comedy Sketch Hall of Fame. At one point in the film, Herschel tangles with Ahmet the Giant in a recreation of the David and Goliath legend,

with Dudley cast as . . . guess who? . . . David. Only this David's fight is less than fair, he shoots the rocks from his slingshot at an extremely vulnerable area of the giant's body, the groin. In another scene, Herschel exposes as a fraud a blindman-beggar's street corner business of collecting money from townspeople.

But once again, Dudley suffered from a lack of substantial material, and was disappointed with how the film turned out. The script runs out of gas once the novelty of the Biblical setting wears off, and when the film has to tell its thin story, the comedy is stifled. As with Dudley's other ill-fated spoof, *BEDAZZLED*, the material would have been better off as a ten-minute sketch. In addition, the film was in the hands of a first time the-

Dudley Moore and Richard "Pharaoh" Pryor confer in "Wholly Moses!"

atrical film director whose sluggish pace further damaged the film. Weis' camera angles were miserably off-target in setting up and executing the gags properly. Finally, the film sadly wasted the performances of its well-known stars. The critical prospects for *WHOLLY MOSES!* were bleak from the day it opened.

Film critics tried taking into account the lack of solidly constructed material when they blasted *WHOLLY MOSES!* in their reviews. As a critic for *DAILY VARIETY*, a Hollywood trade paper, said: ". . .a couple of okay slapstick moments remind us of how funny he (Moore) can be, but in the long run, there's nothing he can do with the material." *HOLLYWOOD REPORTER* likewise determined that the comedy in the film died a quick death when it lamented, "The film unfolds smoothly, but it's ultimately rather dull, due to Weis' undistinctive direction." A stalwart supporter of Moore, however, *BOX OFFICE MAGAZINE* found a glimmer of hope in the production when it wrote that "the slapstick and mugging of Dudley Moore as Herschel help in drawing laughs out of even the flattest material." Although the film's concept deserved some merit, *WHOLLY MOSES!* was yet another example of Hollywood producers with good intentions who lack a sense of knowing when something would be better left unmade.

While the repercussions of *WHOLLY MOSES!* reverberated for some time, Dudley was approached in the meantime about starring in a new film that the late writer Steve Gordon was directing, called *ARTHUR*. Gordon, who died suddenly of a heart attack in late November of 1982, was a protege of Woody Allen's manager, Charles Joffe, and had written *ARTHUR* with an American actor in mind to portray the title role of a millionaire playboy, Arthur Bach. In fact, such stars as James Caan, Al Pacino, Jack Nicholson, and Richard Dreyfuss were considered for the lead role before Paramount, which had produced Gordon's *THE ONE AND ONLY* with Henry Winkler, nixed the entire project. Gordon took the film to Orion Pictures, where the reception was much more to his liking. Immediately, tryouts were held to determine the top star for *ARTHUR* and Moore won the job hands down. As he recalled, "They came to me later that day, following tryouts of other people. I explained to the director that I couldn't possibly do it as an American since I spent half the time trying to get my vowels right."

According to Moore, the script then had to be rewritten to accommodate his version of the character, which pleased him, since he has been wary of producers who develop scripts modeled entirely after him. As Dudley explained:"I always get nervous when people say they're writing something especially for me. I loved the character (Arthur) and thought it was the funniest script I had ever read, even though some changes were necessary with me playing the role. I just loved that man, Arthur. Those scenes in the beginning of me laughing were something else to do. Getting the laughter out of myself was a problem." As viewers will remember, Arthur's infectious laughter was part of the character's charm.

After Dudley was firmly set to do *ARTHUR*, director Gordon added Sir John Gielgud and Liza Minnelli to the roster as Dudley's co-stars. (Gordon had initially considered Sir Alec Guinness and David Niven for Gielgud's role as Hobson, the snobbish butler-guardian to Arthur.) Moore was the one who recommended that Gielgud be actively sought to portray Hobson. "I told Steve Gordon that he was wonderful at comedy, having seen him in English plays. It was terrific to play off him because he has worked *so* much in the theatre."

Budgeted at $7 million, *ARTHUR* commenced production in May of 1979 and had its gala premiere on July 17, 1981 in Hollywood and New York. The chemistry of Moore, Gielgud, and Minnelli seemed to predestine the film for success, but, as producer Joffe explained, success was not so simple. "We didn't know how to advertise the film at first. We had to learn." It was an expensive learning experience; an advertising budget estimated at $4.5 million was necessary to ignite audiences into seeing *ARTHUR.*

The film opened modestly, grossing $2.7 million in 701 theatres during its first weekend. Three weekends later, however, business had tailed off considerably to $2.4 million collected in 630 theaters—a loss of 81 theaters. It looked like *ARTHUR* had begun a mid-summer swoon when favorable word-of-mouth reactions and Moore's blitz of newspaper, radio, and television appearances all struck at once. It didn't take long for *ARTHUR* to quickly earn the title of "blockbuster," setting a fiery pace at box-offices nationwide and reaffirming Dudley's superstar status. During its first 66 days of distribution, the film racked up $46,731,366 at 939 theaters, an unprecedented amount for a comedy. But then, *ARTHUR* wasn't your *ordinary* comedy film.

ARTHUR is an hour and a half of inebriated madness featuring Moore as Arthur Bach, a fun-loving, millionaire playboy whose major weaknesses are constant drink-

ing and a marked unwillingness to grow up.

Bach is considered a thirty-two-year old child, in the eyes of his snooty butler Hobson (John Gielgud), his chauffeur Bitterman (Ted Ross), and his wealthy parents Martha (Geraldine Fitzgerald) and Stanford Bach (Thomas Barbour). Remaining a child wouldn't be all that bad for Arthur were it not for his parents, who plan on giving him a $750 million inheritance if he marries the daughter of a millionaire acquaintance, Burt Johnson (Stephen Elliot). Arthur is unwilling to accept this offer, however. He would rather have fun in his idyllic world of drinking, picking up women, and living his life to the fullest.

The film's first glimpse of Bach introduces him on a wild joyride through downtown New York City, in a limousine driven by Bitterman. He gleefully orders Bitterman to stop alongside a curb where two hookers are soliciting their wares. Arthur tells the girls in a slurry, drunken voice, that he's looking for someone to spend the night with him, and offers the lucky woman $200. A tall, slender prostitute named Gloria (Anne DeSalvo), clad in red hot pants, takes up his offer. Moore then cracks, "Bitterman, please pay the other girl $100 for coming in second!" laughing as he drives off merrily with his lady of the evening.

It is clear to everyone that Arthur is a drunk and that he doesn't even believe that there *is* a state of sobriety. He feeds on alcohol in order to forget his own troubles, the first of which is growing up. His romp through the city lands him and Gloria at the Plaza Hotel, where Arthur exits the limo falling flat on his face. The pratfall is entertaining to Bitterman and Gloria, who break out laughing, but not to the stonefaced hotel onlookers. Inside one of the hotel's posh restaurants, Arthur introduces Gloria to his aunt and uncle, telling them in his blathering

way that she is actually the ruler of a small ("Very little, very tiny, quite small") country the size of Rhode Island. His aunt and uncle take immediate offense at his tipsy behavior, advising him they'll meet again when he's more sober. Arthur escorts Gloria to their table for dinner, where he explains his evening with her will be like New Year's Eve, "the third time this week." With his celebration fun to the last drop of Scotch, Bach takes Gloria back to his lavish, uptown apartment.

The next time Arthur appears is the next morning, thrilling to the choo-choo sounds of his toy train set. Arthur's room is designed like a child's: it contains a miniature basketball court, a dart board, a poster-size picture of himself, a set of trains that ride through a tiny city, his own gold-laden throne—a real rich kid's treasure-chest!

Arthur's chances for more romance with Gloria, who has been an overnight guest, are abruptly halted, however, when Hobson enters with the proper medicine for Arthur's hangover (orange juice, coffee, and aspirin). At first, Hobson appears to be a stereotypical, highly sophisticated servant, dapperly attired in the sort of tuxedo generally fancied by magicians. But he surprises everyone with his outrageously pompous behavior. To the woefully inarticulate Gloria, Hobson says, "I look forward to your next syllable with eagerness." Hobson is more than just Arthur's butler; he acts as a self-appointed guardian as well. Gloria, like the prostitutes before in Arthur's parade of one-night stands, makes a quick exit.

Arthur must next face what he considers to be the worst task of his life; meeting with his crusty old father to discuss his marriage to Susan, the purebred, ultra-sweet daughter of Burt Johnson. Arthur is accompanied by Hobson, who treats Arthur like a child, ordering him to sit up straight and promising him ice cream if he's good. Arthur evidently

Moore, Sir John Gielgud and Liza Minnelli, the award-winning trio from "Arthur," 1981.

has some growing up to do.

The meeting quickly becomes a battle. Arthur doesn't love Susan and sees no reason for marrying someone towards whom he does not feel romantically inclined. His father retorts with one very good reason, that is, the vast sum of money Arthur would receive for marrying the girl. Bull-headed and stubborn, Arthur tells his father where he can put the marriage and his money, and stalks out of the office. His father, not missing a beat, quips loudly, "I'm sorry to see you feel that way Arthur, since your inheritance is only $750 million." Arthur who until then didn't realize exactly how massive his inheritance was to be, flies back into the room and without hesitation waxes eloquent about how marvelous a girl Susan really is. "Have you ever seen when the light catches her face just right?" he gladly proclaims. "Of course, you can't depend on that light!" Then, he adds, "And her chicken—she makes the greatest chicken . . . ." trying to convince himself marrying Susan would not be such a catastrophe. Arthur's father sees fit to congratulate his son for finally growing up. Or so he thinks.

Arthur and Hobson then decide to make some pre-marital purchases at one of Manhattan's finest and most expensive clothing stores. While on this shopping spree, Arthur notices a woman wearing an undersized cowboy hat, who appears to be stealing a gray dress tie. He is fascinated, not by her actions but by her natural beauty. The woman scurries out of the store with the pilfered tie but is followed by the store's security man as well as Arthur and Hobson. As the guard starts harassing the woman, Arthur intervenes and explains that the young woman was buying the tie for him. The girl, a struggling actress named Linda Marolla (Liza Minnelli), instantly catches on to Arthur's ploy and interjects how stupid it was of her not to bill the tie

to his account. As Linda shows everyone the tie, Bach feigns absolute love for the item and then gives Linda a big, long smooch. The embarrassed security guard thanks Arthur for his timely explanation and dashes from the scene like a scared puppy dog.

After the incident Arthur confesses to Linda that he's interested in *her*, not some silly tie. He has found what he feels is true love. Linda is understandably suspicious of Arthur, because of his superficial smile and Hobson's mute, cigar-store Indian pose. Instead of continuing the conversation, she tries taking refuge on a bus en route to Queens, where she lives and supports her unemployed father (Barney Martin). Before she is able to board the bus, however, she discovers that Arthur is not only rich, but single as well. Linda then recites her phone number to Arthur, who accepts it readily and immediately invites her to dinner that evening. Hobson, who has remained silent throughout the interchange, now offers a caustic suggestion for Linda as to her choice of wardrobe for the evening to come: "Steal something casual." Linda accepts Arthur's invitation before being chauffeurred home by Bitterman in Arthur's limousine.

But complications arise after the first date. After all, Arthur has to be honest with himself, he is under pressure to marry Susan, he does want the inheritance, and it would be despicable of him to lead Linda along without telling her the truth. He shamefully calls Linda to tell her that he's engaged, bringing both her and her scruffy, jobless father to tears (he's upset at losing the money, not Arthur).

Arthur's next step is to meet with Susan's father to make his official proposal of marriage. Mr. Johnson, an overbearing, easily angered man, warns Arthur that he better make Susan happy since she's his "golden treasure" and should be treated as such.

A dapper Dudley Moore as Arthur Bach in the film "Arthur," 1981.

Johnson confesses that he's killed for lesser reasons, murdering someone when he was eleven for stealing some food. Arthur, stoned drunk, comprehends this warning loud and clear, commenting, "If I make her cranky, you'll probably just break my ankles."

When Susan accepts Arthur's proposal, Johnson stages an unforgettably posh engagement party. And befitting the tear-jerking element of *ARTHUR*, one uninvited guest makes a surprise appearance...Linda Marolla. Hobson had paid her a visit that afternoon urging her to go, recognizing what he called "true love." During this visit, Hobson's voice grew progressively hoarser ,and he coughed uncontrollably to clear his throat. The tender, sentimental story takes a new twist: Hobson is dying. When Linda quizzes

him about his health, he replies, "I have seen a doctor and he has seen me."

As the festivities of the engagement party proceed, Arthur naturally spots Linda among the throng and snatches her away to the horse stables to be alone. During these quiet moments together, he admits he doesn't want to marry Susan but that his family is forcing the issue. Linda understands, though she tries to win Arthur over one final time. Their romantic interlude is cut short, however, when Susan, his fiancee, enters upon the scene, catching Arthur and Linda on the verge of kissing. Linda cleverly devises a way out of this jam by saying that she came to Arthur for money to help support her unemployed husband and ailing son. Overcome with emotion, Susan runs to console Linda

right, **John Gielgud and Dudley Moore in a scene from "Arthur," 1981.**

and then admits her reason for intruding was to inform Arthur that Hobson's been hospitalized.

Grief-stricken, Arthur rushes to the hospital and does everything to aid Hobson in his recuperation, lavishing him with toys and feeding him the finest catered food from New York's best restaurants. His efforts prove fruitless, however, as Hobson dies. Arthur returns to guzzling his old nemesis, alcohol (he had stopped during the week of Hobson's illness), and comes to the realization he must marry Linda, even if a life of poverty kills him. Resplendent in top hat and tuxedo, he swoops down upon Linda at the greasy-spoon eatery where she works part-time, asking her to marry him. He whisks Linda away, and, on the very same day that he is scheduled to marry Susan, they arrange to meet at the chapel.

Arthur's decision to inform Susan, minutes before the wedding, of his intention to marry Linda creates a rather unsightly scene. She screams at the top of her lungs for help from—who else?—her murderously-inclined father. Burt Johnson grabs the diminutive Arthur and pummels him about the room. As the carnage continues, Linda enters to find a bloodied Arthur on the ground, helplessly drunk and in the vengeful clutches of Johnson. With Linda on the scene, Johnson then becomes perversely enamored of the idea of killing them both with a butcher knife. He stalks towards his victims, raising the knife high. But Martha, Arthur's strong and imposing grandmother, arrives in the nick of time, slapping Johnson in the face and warning him, "Don't screw with me, Burt."

Stunning Susan Anton.

The film then dissolves to show an empty church, with Linda tending to Arthur's facial wounds. Still seated in the church, Martha eavesdrops on Arthur's plan to get a job and live the life of poverty with his new bride, Linda. She, however, will hear of no such inanity and offers Arthur the inheritance so as to preserve a family tradition—no Bach has ever had to work.

ARTHUR, one of the most likeable film fantasies to hit the theatre screen in ages, contained the most likable film character Moore has ever portrayed. His child-like demeanor enhanced the overall believability and fantasy of the millionaire playboy trying to grow up. But, best of all, his feigned inebriation scenes were hilarious, and of a winning caliber. Dudley's laugh alone was enough to make audiences howl; while John Gielgud as the wisecracking butler and Liza Minnelli as the star-struck waitress suited their roles

perfectly. Director Steve Gordon did a masterful job of supervising the film (which he also wrote), and Christopher Cross' theme song, *Best That You Can Do*, was lively and relative to the film's underlying message of love not for money but for love's sake. Truly, *ARTHUR* was a team effort.

Critics were unanimous in their support of *ARTHUR*. The *HOLLYWOOD REPORTER* enthused: "One of the things that makes it (*ARTHUR*) all work so well is Moore. His great sense of comedy—including impeccable timing on delivery, business and reaction—gives the picture its momentum and its style. Moore's Arthur is probably the most lovable eccentric since Jimmy Stewart's Elwood P. Dowd in *HARVEY*. Vincent Canby of *THE NEW YORK TIMES* also jumped on the bandwagon when he trumpeted the following praise: "Mr. Moore is, if possible, more uninhibitedly comic than he was in Blake Edwards' *10*. His Arthur is a satyr, a sprite, an over-age waif and a consistently endearing showoff. His timing is magical." Critics likewise spoke highly of Sir John Gielgud as Hobson. The *HOLLYWOOD REPORTER* wrote; "Moore's main competition as top banana, though, is John Gielgud, who is absolutely wonderful as Arthur's valet-nanny friend."

ARTHUR stormed up a worldwide business, grossing over $77 million. At the same time, Dudley found himself caught in a different kind of current, a romantic one, that also created an international stir. Moore's latest romance was with the leggy singer-dancer-actress, Susan Anton (who at 6 feet stands almost a foot taller than Moore), and the press corps would not let go of the picturesque couple. Moore was disturbed by the media hype over his relationship with Anton, which initially sprang into the public eye two months before the release of *ARTHUR*. As he commented at the time, "It's sexual vo-

yeurism. People seem to get a curious, vicarious thrill about the sexual wanderings of celebrities. It's quite ludicrous, yet I'm delighted they're interested as well."

Dudley had to learn how to balance the demands of his status with his desire to lead a private life with Susan. With his divorce from Tuesday Weld now official (she gained custody of their son, Patrick, and a division of their mutual community property), Dudley wanted his future romances to remain in the confines of his personal life. With Anton at his side, Moore began feeling comfortable for the first time in his life. Susan possessed the ability to communicate openly with him on her feelings about him, her expectations of their relationship and, above all, had deep respect for Dudley's privacy.

Anton first became a nationally recognized face in 1976 when she replaced Edie Adams as the Muriel Cigar girl. Shortly

thereafter, television's onetime-master-programmer Fred Silverman spotted her and subsequently cast her with Mel Tillis in a tongue-in-cheek series called *CLIFFHANGERS*, and then her own variety show. Even though none of the programs was successful, a film offer and album contracts were forthcoming, so the future was bright all the same. Besides, Susan's sultry blonde hair, unblemished complexion, and shapely, fashion model figure attracted continual attention from magazines and newspapers. Gossip mongers and the insatiable appetite of the press had hounded her until the novelty of her celebrity status began to wear off. She was able to relate, therefore, to Moore's request that his life retain some degree of privacy. The couple has contemplated marriage for some time—they have been together for more than two years—but is not rushing it.

Susan once described what drew her to

The late Steve Gordon and Dudley Moore on the set of "Arthur," 1981.

Dudley: "He just made me feel good and happy, just watching him. I thought it was time to be around a person who puts out a positive vibration. I think Dudley's main attraction is that he's very secure and positive about his life, therefore his understanding of other people is very attractive. You want to tell him every secret you ever had."

The excitement of a new romance coincided with a hiatus following *ARTHUR* that gave Moore the chance to play the piano at home much more regularly than he had been doing. He had become inspired to perform in public again, and, as he confessed in an interview at the time, "I'm creeping back. I'm not sure how much of it I want to do, because it's such hard work. You have to have some kind of athletic approach to playing an instrument. It's very boring because I get so lazy when it comes to that."

Dudley convinced himself that he should add an occasional public performance to his rigorous schedule. So, in the summer months of 1981, Moore performed brilliantly in several musical concerts, first with the Los Angeles Philharmonic and then with several other distinguished classical musicians at The New York Metropolitan Museum of Art. Musicgoers were spellbound by his performance, beckoning for encore after encore. It seemed as if anything Dudley touched turned instantly to gold; his music, his film career, and his love life, were all at a zenith never before known to him.

Moore continued at this breakneck pace for months. His acting peers elected him best actor (for *ARTHUR*) at the annual Golden Globe awards. Meanwhile, his agent, Lou Pitt, closed four exclusive feature film deals, all commencing production within months of each other.

One of Moore's exclusive picture deals was to film *ROMANTIC COMEDY*, featuring Mary Steenburgen, who won the

Best Supporting Actress Oscar in 1980 for *MELVIN AND HOWARD*. Directed by Arthur Hiller, *ROMANTIC COMEDY* began production in early June and is an adaptation of the 1979 Broadway show hit of the same title. Moore is cast in the role of a playwright who teams with another writer (Steenburgen) to work on several ambitious projects, during which time they become romantically involved. As in *10*, with Bo Derek, Moore appears in another nude scene, this time with a bare chested Mary Steenburgen. In discussing the scene, Dudley said, "We meet nude. When I first meet Mary, I mistake her for a masseuse, so I drop my drawers." But *ROMANTIC COMEDY* is not intended to be as silly and wacky as *ARTHUR*, a film, in any case, which Dudley may be hard-pressed to top. Instead, Moore took on the project because the script contained more verbal than visual humor, which he considers his forte. As he explained: "It's got a lot of dialogue. Very witty. It's a well-scripted comedy and I love dialogue stuff. More so than sitting in a plane doing reaction shots to spaceships whizzing by. I like to play people who aren't idiots. It's nice to play characters who are like myself."

Moore's next screen role was in *SIX WEEKS*, co-starring Mary Tyler Moore. Filming commenced on November 16, 1981 and concluded on January 19, 1982, with location shooting taking place in New York and Hollywood. Jon Peters, Barbara Streisand's beau, produced the film for Polygram Pictures at a budget of $9 million, and Tony Bill, who co-produced *THE STING* and *TAXI DRIVER*, directed. It was only Bill's first feature as a director.

Based on a novel by Fred Mustard Stewart, and a screenplay by David Seltzer (who wrote *THE OTHER SIDE OF THE MOUNTAIN* and *THE OMEN*), the film is "a bittersweet romance" which revolves around

Dudley Moore performing Gershwin with the Los Angeles Philharmonic at Hollywood Bowl in California, Summer 1981.

Dudley Moore as a hopeful congressional candidate in "Six Weeks," 1982.

the love affair between a married Congressional candidate, Patrick Dalton (Dudley Moore), and a snobbish head of a cosmetics firm, Charlotte Dreyfus (Mary Tyler Moore), and the mother of a twelve-year-old daughter (Katherine Healy), who is dying from leukemia. In the last six weeks of her life, thus explaining the film's title, Healy longs for a father to call her own. Moore fills that bill for a time.

SIX WEEKS is a sentimental film which marks Dudley's first semi-dramatic performance. The film's ending is clearly a tear-jerker, with Moore saying good-bye to Mary Tyler Moore at the international terminal at John F. Kennedy Airport in New York City.

But the ending is not as saccharin as such conclusions usually are, contends director Bill. As he told a reporter during production, "There is no question, the film runs the risk of being sentimental. But it's not my style and I'm going against that possibility at all times. Like this scene now, Dudley and Mary are saying final goodbyes to each other after a last magical weekend in New York. It's what I call a standard movie scene, the kind that can easily become two characters giving each other a tearful goodbye, then turning around, making eye contact, and running into each other's arms one last time. I'm constantly aware of the possibility of that sort of egregious miscalculation."

Moore, Katherine Healy and Mary Tyler Moore from "Six Weeks," 1982.

Dudley has said that he thoroughly enjoyed making the picture and having the opportunity to play his character in a naturalistic way. As he said, "I play my character just as I'm talking to you. I don't believe in sitting in a bucket of ice water for six months to soak up the traits of a character. An actor is most convincing when he injects himself into his role. After doing caricatures for the past three years, this film is a luxury for me."

Nevertheless, as with *10* and *ARTHUR*, Moore was faced with some rather awkward situations during the filming of *SIX WEEKS*. As he recalled: "In one scene, Mary and I are supposed to be having a quiet moment with each other in the open air, and when I looked overhead, there were 50 bystanders watching me. But, with all the pressure, the work on this film has not been exhausting."

Dudley's second film out of the four-picture deal, *LOVESICK*, commenced production immediately afterwards in early February. It co-stars Sir Alec Guinness and Elizabeth McGovern (from *RAGTIME)* in a contemporary comedy which has Moore as a psychoanalyst seeking advice from Sigmund Freud (Guinness) about his affair with a patient (McGovern). If this strikes some folks as similar to *PLAY IT AGAIN, SAM*'s use of Humphrey Bogart, that may be because the director of *LOVESICK* is Marshall Brickman, known for his collaborations with Woody Allen and his own film, *SIMON*. *LOVESICK* was produced by the Ladd Company, headed by the son of the late actor Alan Ladd.

According to his co-workers, Moore pulled several practical jokes on the cast and crew to help boost morale and keep spirits high. Jeff Natter, who makes his film debut in *LOVESICK*, remembered in an interview one of Dudley's pranks: "Dudley kept everyone in stitches by walking around with a box in his pocket that made farting noises. He'd walk up to the actresses, then the box would make its sound and then he'd say, 'I can't believe that *you* did that. Do apologize.'"

That's not to say that Moore's associates didn't get even—Dudley was made to laugh at himself as well. During one incident director Brickman displayed his own quick-wittedness by preying on one of Dudley's weaknesses. As Natter explained: "Dudley made one of his entrances and Marshall Brickman said, 'You have to move to the center of the camera frame, you look a little small.' Dudley said, 'Well, if you'd like an actor of larger stature, that's all right.' And he walked off the set."

Moore received some good news during the filming of *LOVESICK*. The Academy of Motion Picture Arts and Sciences had nominated him along with the late Henry Fonda, Burt Lancaster, and Warren Beatty for the best actor Oscar. One month before the 54th Annual Academy Awards was telecast Dudley appeared with song-writer Christopher Cross on the ABC television Actors' Fund of America special, *NIGHT OF 100 STARS*, performing *ARTHUR*'s theme. Cross sang along while Moore soloed on the piano. But the Academy Awards show was the most prominent on his mind. Dudley had never been nominated for such a prestigious award in all his life, but he was realistic about his chances. On April 15, 1982, the night of the show, Moore escorted Susan Anton, garbed in a slinky, silk dress, to the Dorothy Chandler Pavilion in Los Angeles, where the ceremonies were being held. Outside, Moore was interviewed by *HOLLYWOOD REPORTER* columnist Army Archerd on the Oscar nomination. Dudley said, "Everybody's asking how I am feeling. I feel a certain way about the category and what is going to happen, so I don't feel really nervous."

Dudley certainly had no reason to be. Fonda was the inside favorite to win the

award, with his age and failing health contributing to his chances. The actor, who died in August, 1982, had played his last role in ON GOLDEN POND, and despite riveting performances in many films, had never won an Oscar. It was a sure bet that Fonda would win.

He did. Daughter Jane accepted the Oscar on her father's behalf, (since Henry was by then too ill to appear at the ceremonies). At a cast party afterwards Moore was asked to sum up his loss. He admitted, with the humility and praise that mark the true Hollywood professional, "I'm delighted that Fonda won. I think it's just great. I expected him to win. And I would have been really slightly uncomfortable if by some chance I had won."

Shortly after the Oscars, strange rumors began circulating through the Hollywood grapevine that Moore was dropping his lover, Susan Anton, for his LOVESICK co-star Elizabeth McGovern. The story broke on May 4, 1982 when the LOVESICK cast threw a party for the production at Manhattan's Central Falls restaurant, and it was reported that Dudley and Liz spent most of the evening smooching behind a pillar. But such gossip seemed more like a press agent's scheme to hype Moore's forthcoming movie. In fact, Dudley was still seeing Anton. The actress was arrested for drunk driving over Memorial Day weekend driving Moore's Rolls Royce; while this was rather inauspicious confirmation that the relationship was still thriving, Dudley and Susan do indeed continue their relationship. The two headlined a 1982 fundraising event in Hollywood for the American Diabetes Association, and truly show no signs that they've wearied in their affections for each other.

Dudley's next picture slated for production was UNFAITHFULLY YOURS, a remake of the 1948 Preston Sturges comedy that starred Rex Harrison. In the new version, Moore plays a famous conductor married to a much younger woman of whom he's insanely jealous. The film started shooting in January, 1983, with Howard Zieff directing from a Valerie Curtin-Barry Levinson screenplay. Moore's salary for the film was a healthy $2.5 million, plus percentages of the box office revenue.

Dudley's biggest conquest of the year came in August, 1982, when his newest album, SMILIN' THROUGH, featuring vocalist Cleo Laine, was issued. It marked the first time Moore had played opposite Laine since he originally joined the John Dankworth band in 1960. (Laine is Dankworth's wife). In reviewing the disc, LOS ANGELES TIMES jazz critic Leonard Feather wrote: "That Moore has kept up his piano chops is engagingly demonstrated here. There are Errol Garner touches in some of his solos, but on the Alec Wilder melody, 'Be a Child,' his sensitivity is evocative of Bill Evans. Given the tasteful mix of old and new material, this stacks up as a 4¼-star surprise."

But Dudley should no longer be a surprise to anyone. It is obvious that he measures up well in any medium: movies, television, orchestral stage, and recordings. His one goal has been to entertain. And with the ease and grace of Marcel Marceau, the deadpan manner of Peter Sellers and Buster Keaton, and, most importantly, a style all his own, he has done just that. With a string of popular successes behind him, and a full roster of projects and offers ahead, Dudley's popularity and appeal should only grow.

Moore and the beauteous Mary Steenburgen on the set of "Romantic Comedy."

CHAPTER 7

"Moore on Moore"

Equally important as Dudley Moore, the comedian, is Dudley Moore, the man. To a casual viewer, Dudley has everything a man usually wants out of life: success, women, money, and fame. But a deeper look at Dudley reveals that his emotions are still wounded from two disastrous marriages and from enduring the struggles with himself, a battle that has, finally, put his identity problems behind him. Success, it seems, has made Dudley come to terms with reality, and, at last, himself.

Moore moved to Los Angeles in 1979 when his career really started to take off. He viewed the change of venue as a fresh start, a cleansing of his past. As he remarked about living in one of the smoggiest cities in the world, "I like it here. I've been a professional for over 21 years and yet this is sort of a new start over here." To move to the United States Dudley shipped from London 71 cases of books, records, and bedsteads. It would appear that Dudley is in Los Angeles on a permanent basis. Moore settled into a modest beachfront house overlooking the community of Marina Del Rey, located on a small strip of California landfill. His constant com-

panion (besides Susan) is his faithful miniature Pekinese dog, Kong. Beside the sparkling, dark blue water of the Pacific Ocean, Marina Del Rey is the perfect place for a girl-watcher like Moore. The expanse of sand dunes has its share of healthy distractions; girls strolling along in bikinis, women joggers scantily clad in high-cut shorts. (Not that Dudley needs any women besides Susan Anton, it's just that he has always preferred to live where the scenery is pleasant.)

His living room is adorned with an outsized grand piano, elaborate stereo equipment, and, tucked among his books, a framed photograph of his son, Patrick, whom he visits often. Alongside that portrait, Moore has posted an eyecatching shot of himself decked out in a V-neck sweater and open collar shirt, surrounded by twenty-one men and women, all totally nude. This was the cast of pornographic film actors hired to appear in the orgy scene with him in *10*, a sequence he is said to regret.

Dudley considers himself a perfectionist of the highest order when it comes to his personal life and his work, and thus he is pretty sensitive to what critics say. In fact, he has composed his own "hit list" of English and American critics who have lambasted his performances in film. "I'm not paranoid, but I feel personally hurt when English reviewers attack me unnecessarily," Moore said in an interview. "So I've taken to writing back to them." For instance, Dudley once remarked that one woman reviewing *10* complained that men were treated to Bo Derek while women had to settle for "a middle-age, dwarf-sized man with a squeaky voice.'" Moore's reply to this female critic was unprintable, though he suggested she send him a photograph of herself for his appraisal.

Moore realizes that in his profession criticism comes with success. He's not so sure, however, that he would have been able

to emotionally handle such situations earlier in his career. He admitted, "If this had happened, say, 25 years ago, I'd have acted differently. I'd probably have retreated into a character instead of being myself. In spite of it all, I feel untrammelled. The anticipation that might have arisen is very much less feverish than I thought it would have been."

Dudley feels he probably worked harder at the start of his career, to firmly establish himself in his field, than he does now. The frenetic pace he had undertaken during those crucial years was enough to exhaust anyone, including himself. Today, Dudley claims that he puts very little energy into preparing for his screen roles. "I'd have to say I was remaking myself and thus sort of inserting myself into the script, rather than looking for

anything too far away from me. I feel I can produce more vulnerabilty when I work from myself, as if it were, literally, to put on a red nose or mask," he explained.

His manner of acting is strictly non-Method (meaning the intensive character immersion and role study taught by the late Lee Strasberg). He says, "I don't research or study. I get into the role ten seconds before the camera rolls and when the camera stops, I get off. I like to work on a platform of ease. I don't want a big heavy challenge that means you have to pull something out of yourself which may not be natural. I want the opportunity to explore, but as I like to do it."

About his funny side, Moore remarked, "I think of comedy as reflecting feelings, satirizing them. I frankly find it hard to define

right, **Dudley Moore leaving Heathrow airport on his way to Los Angeles, 1981.**

left, **Dudley Moore in high spirits as Arthur Bach from the film "Arthur," 1981.**

myself, because I always think of comedians as people who stand up and tell jokes. I couldn't do that for one moment. I've even proved it."

Moore's audiences identify him with physical comedians from the Golden Age of Comedy like Chaplin, Keaton, the Marx Brothers, and with Peter Sellers, of British and American fame, and it is a technique which he takes great pride in performing. As Moore told critic Charles Champlin in a television interview, "Some people almost take physical comedy for granted. Some people tell me that I am a physical comedian. And I say, 'I am?' I am not being curt about it, but I have always assumed that you have to be physical, in some way or another. I am not physical in the same caricature as I used to be. In the last films *10* and *ARTHUR*, I have found a much more naturalistic pace. But I used a lot of physical comedy only because I had always done it."

Dudley has not always looked for good stories and definable characters in movies, however. In some of his earliest British film productions, for example, the main drawbacks were lack of character definition and improperly woven stories. Today, he wouldn't find that acceptable. As he puts it: "A story with a comedy is important. Then the comedy has legs. That's why I think jokey comedies—for instance *ANIMAL HOUSE* won't last. You don't sympathize with the characters. You need a character you warm to."

Dudley believes that his film characters contain all the important ingredients like sincerity, compassion, and a good sense of humor. "I have the ability to believe totally in the work I'm doing. I'm honest, vulnerable and not afraid to show my feelings. I think what I am as a person is very positive for an audience to see. I sincerely want to make people happy. I enjoy making audiences laugh.

Sex appeal is very important to an actor who wants to be a star. I know I'll never affect women the way Robert Redford does, but I'm having fun stumbling in his footsteps." While his fans might disagree with this self-deprecating assessment, Moore appears to be handling his own sex symbol status rather nicely.

Of his two failed marriages and his romance with Susan Anton, Moore commented upon what made each relationship a different challenge for him. "With Suzy, I was very repressed, very contained in myself, but I know that she knew all that was going inside me, and didn't have to comment on it. She, in a sense, let me be me. She believed in her own feelings, which I think is something I've just started to learn how to do, to believe in my own feelings," he confessed.

Dudley found that his spells of silent moods presented some personal obstacles for him when he married Tuesday Weld. "I think the situation with Tuesday was she was somebody who was more agitated about my silences and wanted to pull things out of me, to get the truth out of me."

Moore characterizes himself as a chronic thinker, a loner, a man of quiet notions. One reason his romantic partnership with Susan Anton has worked so well is that she is instrumental in helping Dudley to break out of his introversion. "With Susan, I'm really trying to open up and confront my anger and what I feel. This is something I would have found very difficult to do in the past. I think the reason we get closer all the time is that we confront each other with our feelings. We have confrontations, but we deal with them, and we see beyond them, beyond what is actually behind what we said, realizing what is being felt."

While his intimacy is of paramount importance, Dudley just wants his life to be as uncomplicated as possible. He wants to enjoy each day to the highest degree, and his career goals are certain. He has a burning desire to entertain and make people laugh. Certainly, while filmgoers thrive on him, beckon for him, and laugh with him, Dudley will be successful with all of his ventures.

THE
COMPLETE
WORKS

BEYOND THE FRINGE (Theater Revue)

First performance in Edinburgh, 1960
First performance in London, May 10, 1961
First performance in America, on Broadway in New York City,
October 27, 1962
Producer: Alexander H. Cohen
Staged by: Mr. Cohen
Original London Production directed by Eleanor Fazan
Setting by John Wyckham
Lighting by Ralph Alswang
Cast: Alan Bennett
     Peter Cook
     Dudley Moore
     Jonathan Miller

NOT ONLY. . .BUT ALSO

The BBC television series that debuted January 9, 1965 and ran for several successful seasons. *NOT ONLY. . .BUT ALSO* featured Dudley and Peter in a crazy array of characters and sketches, but none more popular and eagerly received than those incomparable luminaries, "Pete" and "Dud". . . (overleaf)

GUEST APPEARANCES

Top, IT'S LULU, NOT TO MENTION DUDLEY MOORE, *and bottom*, THE BODY IN QUESTION, the science special with old friend and host Jonathan Miller explaining to Dudley how the hand and brain coordinate in piano playing.

Top, BUT SERIOUSLY—IT'S SHEILA HANCOCK, a variety show featuring the British singer, *and bottom,* AN APPLE A DAY, a black comedy written by John Antrobus (who penned the screenplay of The Bed Sitting Room).

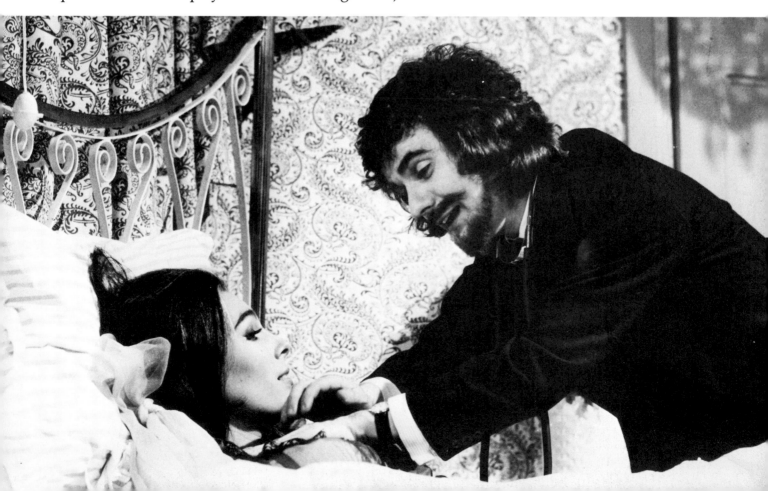

GOOD EVENING (Theater Revue)

First performance in England as Behind the Fridge, November 1972
First performance in America, on Broadway in New York City,
November 1973
Producer: Alexander H. Cohen & Bernard Delfont
       in association with Donald Langdon for Hemdale, LTD.
Director: Jerry Adler
Designer: Robert Randolph
Cast: Peter Cook
    Dudley Moore

FILMOGRAPHY

THE WRONG BOX
Release: July 19, 1966
105 minutes
Salamander Film Productions
Dist: Columbia Pictures
Producer-Director: Bryan Forbes
Screenplay: Larry Gelbart
Photography: Gerry Turpin
Music: Clifford Bevan
Cast: John Mills (Masterman Finsbury)
     Ralph Richardson: (Joseph Finsbury)
     Michael Caine: (Michael)
     Peter Cook: (Morris)
     Dudley Moore: (John)
     Nanette Newman: (Julia)
     Tony Hancock: (detective)
     Peter Sellers: (Doctor Pratt)
     Cicely Courtneidge: (Major Martha)
     Wilfrid Lawson: (Peacock)
     Thorley Walters: (Lawyer Patience)

BEDAZZLED

Release: December 10, 1967
107 minutes
Stanley Donen Enterprises
Dist: Twentieth Century Fox
Producer-Director: Stanley Donen
Story: Peter Cook, Dudley Moore
Screenplay: Peter Cook
Photography: Austin Dempster
Music by Peter Cook and Dudley Moore
Cast: Peter Cook: (George Spiggot)
     Dudley Moore: (Stanley Moon)
     Eleanor Bron: (Margaret Spencer)
     Raquel Welch: (Lillian Lust)
     Alba: (Vanity)
     Rob Russell: (Anger)
     Barry Humphries: (Envy)
     Parnell McGarry: (Glutton)
     Daniele Noel: (Avarice)
     Howard Goorney: (Sloth)
     Michael Bates: (Inspector Clarke)
     Bernard Spear: (Irving Moses)
     Robin Hawdon: (Randolph)
     Michael Trubshawe: (Lord Dowdy)
     Evelyn Moore: (Mrs. Wisby)
     Lockwood West: (Saint Peter)
     Betty Cooper: (Sister Pheobe)
     Peter Hutchins: (P.C. Roberts)

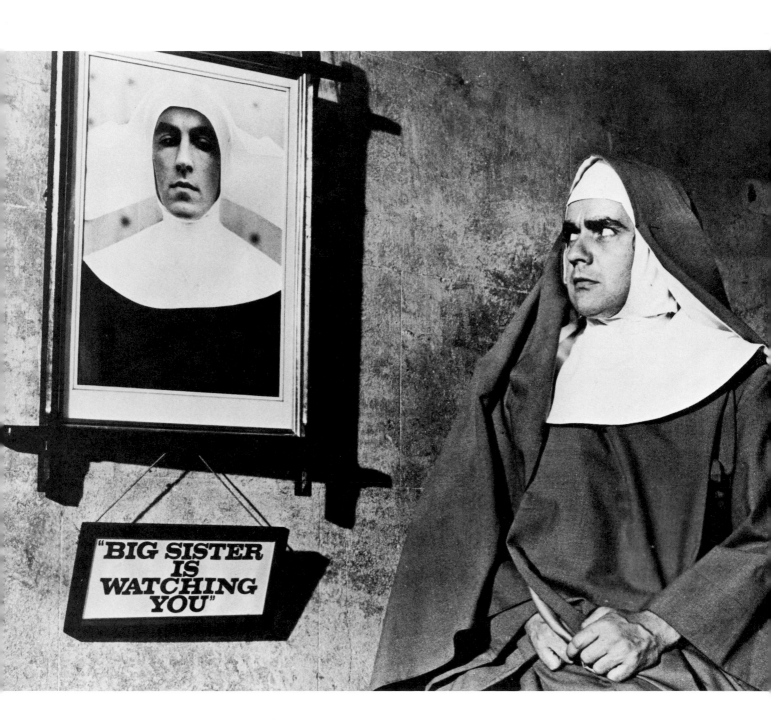

119

30 IS A DANGEROUS AGE CYNTHIA

Release: March 4, 1968
85 minutes
Walter Shenson Films
Dist: Columbia Pictures
Producer: Walter Shenson
Director: Joseph McGrath
Screenplay: Dudley Moore, Joseph McGrath, and John Wells
Photography: Billy Williams
Music: Dudley Moore
Cast: Dudley Moore (Rupert Street)
    Eddie Foy, Jr. (Oscar)
    Suzy Kendall (Louise Hammond)
    John Bird (Herbert Greenslade)
    Duncan Macrae (Jock McCue)
    Patricia Routledge (Mrs. Woolley)
    Peter Bayliss (Victor)
    John Wells (Hon. Gavin Hopton)
    Harry Towb (Mr. Woolley)
    Jonathan Routh (Captain Gore-Taylor)
    Ted Dicks (Horst Cohen, Jr.)
    Nicky Henson (Paul)
    Clive Dunn (Doctor)
    Frank Thornton (registrar)
    Derek Farr (television announcer)
    Michael MacLiammoir (Irish storyteller)
    The Dudley Moore Trio

THOSE DARING YOUNG MEN IN THEIR JAUNTY JALOPIES

Release: May 29, 1969
122 minutes
A Ken Annakin Film
Dist: Paramount Pictures
Producer-Director: Ken Annakin
Screenplay: Jack Davies, Ken Annakin
Photography: Gabor Pogany
Music: Ron Goodwin
Cast: Tony Curtis (Chester Shofield)
     Susan Hampshire (Betty)
     Terry-Thomas (Sir Cuthbert Ware-Armitage)
     Eric Sykes (Perkins)
     Gert Frobe (Otto)
     Peter Cook (Major Digby Dawlish)
     Dudley Moore (Lieutenant Kit Barrington)
     Walter Chiari (Angelo Pincelli)
     Lando Buzzanca (Marcello Agosti)
     Mireille Darc (Marie-Claude)
     Marie Dubois (Pasquale)
     Nicoletta Machiavelli (Dominique)
     Bourvil (Monsieur Vendredi)

THE BED SITTING ROOM

Release: September 28, 1969
90 minutes
Oscar Lewenstein Productions
Dist: Lopert Pictures/United Artists
Producer-Director: Richard Lester
Screenplay: John Antrobus
Photography: David Watkin
Music: Ken Thorne
Cast: Rita Tushingham (Penelope)
     Ralph Richardson (Lord Fortnum)
     Peter Cook (police Inspector)
     Dudley Moore (police Sergeant)
     Spike Milligan (Mate)
     Richard Warwick (Alan)
     Michael Hordern (Capt. Bules Martin)
     Roy Kinnear (Plastic Mac Man)
     Arthur Lowe (father)
     Mona Washbourne (mother)
     Ronald Fraser (The Army)
     Dandy Nichols (Mrs. Ethel Shroake)
     Frank Thornton (The BBC)
     Harry Secombe (Shelter Man)
     Jimmy Edwards (Nigel)
     Henry Woolf (electricity man for the entire nation)
     Jack Sheperd (underwater Vicar)
     Marty Feldman (Nurse Arthur)
     Bill Wallis (The Prime Minister)
     Gordon Rollings (deep feed patient)
     Ronnie Brody (dwarf chauffeur)
     Cecil Cheng (Chinaman)
     Eddie Malin (club waiter)
     Chris Konyils (policeman)
     Ron Moody (as himself)

ALICE'S ADVENTURES IN WONDERLAND

Release: November 8, 1972
96 minutes
A Rainbow Adventure Fim
Dist: American International Pictures
Producer: Derek Horne
Director: William Sterling
Screenplay: William Sterling
Photograpy: Geoff Unsworth
Music: John Barry
Cast: Fiona Fullerton (Alice)
     Michael Crawford (White Rabbit)
     Ralph Richardson (Caterpillar)
     Flora Robson (Queen of Hearts)
     Peter Sellers (March Hare)
     Robert Helpmann (Mad Hatter)
     Dudley Moore (Doormouse)
     Michael Jayston (Dodgson)
     Spike Milligan (Gryplton)

127

FOUL PLAY

Release: July 6, 1978
116 minutes
A Colin Higgins Film
Dist: Paramount Pictures
Producers: Thomas L. Miller, Edward K. Milkis
Director-writer: Colin Higgins
Photography: David M. Walsh
Music: Charles Fox
Cast: Goldie Hawn (Gloria Mundy)
  Chevy Chase (Det. Tony Carlson)
  Burgess Meredith (Landlord Hennesey)
  Rachel Roberts (Gerda Casswell)
  Eugene Roche (Archbishop)
  Dudley Moore (Stanley Tibbets)
  Bruce Solomon (Det. Scott)
  Marilyn Sokol (Stella)
  Brian Dennehy (Det. Fergie)
  Chuck McCann (Theatre Manager)
  Billy Barty (Religious Salesman)
  Don Calfa (Scarface)
  Marc Lawrence (Stiltskin)
  Cooper Huckabee (Sandy)
  William Frankfather (Albino)
  Ian Teadoescu (Turk)
  Pat Ast (Massage Parlour Madame)
  John Hancock (Coleman)
  Queenie Smith (Elsie)
  Hope Summers (Ethel)
  Cyril Magnin (Pope Pius XIII)
  Irene Tedrow (Mrs. Monk)
  Chuck Walsh (Newscaster)

THE HOUND OF THE BASKERVILLES

Release: November 1, 1978
84 minutes
A Paul Morrisey Film
Dist: Hemdale International Films
Producer: John Goldstone
Director: Paul Morrisey
Screenplay: Peter Cook, Dudley Moore, and Paul Morrisey
Photography: Dick Bush, John Wilcox
Music: Dudley Moore
Cast: Peter Cook (Sherlock Holmes)
     Dudley Moore (Dr. Watson)
     Denholm Elliot (Stapleton)
     Joan Greenwood (Beryl Stapleton)
     Terry-Thomas (Dr. Mortimer)
     Max Wall (Mr. Barrymore)
     Irene Handl (Mrs. Barrymore)
     Kenneth Williams (Sir Henry Baskerville)
     Hugh Griffith (Frankland)
     Dudley Moore (Mrs. Holmes/Mr. Spiggot)
     Dana Gillespie (Mary)
     Roy Kinnear (Seldon)
     Pruneila Scales (Glynis)
     Penelope Keith (Massage Parlour Receptionist)
     Spike Milligan (Baskerville Police Force)

10
Release: October 5, 1979
113 minutes
A Blake Edwards Film
Dist: Orion Pictures
Producers: Blake Edwards, Tony Adams
Director: Blake Edwards
Screenplay: Blake Edwards
Photography: Frank Stanley
Music: Henry Mancini
Cast: Dudley Moore (George)
    Julie Andrews (Sam)
    Bo Derek (Jenny)
    Robert Webber (Hugh)
    Dee Wallace (Mary Lewis)
    Sam Jones (David)

WHOLLY MOSES!

Release: June 11, 1980
109 minutes
A David Begelman Film
Dist: Columbia Pictures
Producer: Freddie Fields
Director: Gary Weis
Screenplay: Guy Thomas
Photography: Frank Stanley
Music: Patrick Williams
Cast: Dudley Moore (Harvey/Herschel)
        Laraine Newman (Zoey/Serelda)
        Jame Coco (Hyssop)
        Paul Sand (Angel of the Lord)
        Jack Gilford (Tailor)
        Dom DeLuise (Shadroch)
        John Houseman (Archangel)
        Madeline Kahn (Sorceress)
        David L. Lander (Beggar)
        Richard Pryor (Pharoah)
        John Ritter (Devil)

ARTHUR

Release: July 17, 1981
96 minutes
Dist: Orion Pictures through Warner Bros.
Producer: Robert Greenhut
Director: Steve Gordon
Screenplay: Steve Gordon
Photography: Fred Schuler
Music: Burt Bacharach
Cast: Dudley Moore (Arthur Bach)
      Liza Minnelli (Linda Marolla)
      John Gielgud (Hobson)
      Geraldine Fitzgerald (Martha Bach)
      Jill Elkenberry (Susan Johnson)
      Stephen Elliott (Burt Johnson)
      Ted Ross (Bitterman)
      Barney Martin (Ralph Morolla)
      Thomas Barbour (Stanford Bach)
      Anne DeSalvo (Gloria)
      Marjorie Barnes (Hooker)
      Dillion Evans (Oak Room Maitre D')
      Maurice Copeland (Uncle Peter)
      Justina Johnson (Aunt Pearl)

SIX WEEKS

Release: December 17, 1982
107 minutes
Polygram Pictures
Dist: Universal Studios
Producers: Peter Guber & Jon Peters
Director: Tony Bill
Screenplay: David Seltzer
Based on the novel by: Fred Mustard Stewart
Photography: Michael D. Margulies, A.S.C.
Music: Dudley Moore
Art Director: Hilyard Brown
Film Editor: Stu Linder
Cast: Dudley Moore (Patrick Dalton)
     Mary Tyler Moore (Charlotte Dreyfus)
     Katherine Healy (Nicole Dreyfus)
     Shannon Wilcox (Peg Dalton)
     Bill Calvert (Jeff Dalton)
     Joe Regalbuto (Bob Crowther)
     John Harkins (Arnold Stillman)

DISCOGRAPHY

BEYOND THE FRINGE '64
(Capitol/W2072/1964)

NOT ONLY PETER COOK...BUT ALSO DUDLEY MOORE
(Decca/LKA-4703/1965)

BEDAZZLED
(London Records/1966)

L.S. BUMBLE BEE
(Decca U.K./12551/January 1967)

TODAY—With Dudley Moore Trio
(Atlantic/K40397/1972)

GOOD EVENING—With Peter Cook
(Island Records/ILPS 9298/1973)

DEREK AND CLIVE (LIVE)
(Island Records/ILPS 9434/U.K. Release/1976)

DEREK AND CLIVE COME AGAIN
(Virgin Records/V2094/U.K. Release/1977)

DEREK AND CLIVE AD NAUSEUM
(Virgin Records/V2112/U.K. Release/1978)

THE WORLD OF DUDLEY MOORE
(Decca U.K./SPA 286-E)

SMILIN' THROUGH—With Cleo Laine
(Finesse/FW38091/1982)

About The Author:

JEFF LENBURG is a freelance writer of trade biographies and film histories, with a special emphasis on comedy and animated cartoons. Lenburg's credits include THE ENCYCLOPEDIA OF ANIMATED CARTOON SERIES (Arlington House Publishers), which has been nominated for an 1981 American Library Association award; STEVEN MARTIN: THE UNAUTHORIZED BIOGRAPHY (St. Martin's Press); THE THREE STOOGES SCRAPBOOK (Citadel Press), with Greg Lenburg and Joan Maurer (daugher of the three stooges leader, Moe Howard); THE GREAT MOVIE CARTOON DIRECTORS (McFarland and Co.); and DUSTIN HOFFMAN; HOLLYWOOD'S ANTI-HERO (St. Martin's Press).

Lenburg has also contribued a profile of the Three Stooges for CLOSE-UPS: THE MOVIE STAR BOOK (Edited by Danny Peary/Workman Publishing, 1978). He contributed research for three books by Richard Lamparski WHATEVER BECAME OF. . . .? 2ND GIANT ANNUAL (Bantam, 1977); David Ragan's WHO'S WHO IN HOLLYWOOD (Arlington House, 1976); Chris Costello's LOU'S ON FIRST (St. Martin's Press, 1981), a biography of the late comedian Lou Costello; THE BEST AND NEWEST OF WHATEVER BECAME OF. . .? (Crown, 1982), and LAMPARSKI'S HIDDEN HOLLYWOOD, II (Fireside, 1982).

Lenburg has also appeared four times on Boston radio's WITS TRIVIA TALK show, fielding listener's trivia questions about animated cartoons; on RKO Radio Network's nationally syndicated program AMERICAN OVERNIGHT; NBC's THE TODAY SHOW and on many television talk programs in Los Angeles.